Negotiate Like a Boss

Persuasion skills and negotiation techniques

Steven T. Walker

Galatea Editions

Negotiate like a Boss. Persuasion skills and negotiation techniques, by Steven T. Walker.

© Steven T. Walker 2021
© Galatea Editions 2021
© All rights reserved.

Thank you for buying this book. Copyright is the exclusive property of the author. Its reproduction, copying or distribution is not allowed whether for commercial or non-profit purposes.

Index

- **INTRODUCTION** ... 9
- **ABOUT PERSUASION** ... 13
  - What is persuasion? ... 13
- **THE PSYCHOLOGICAL LAWS OF PERSUASION** ... 17
  - Persuasion by sympathy ... 18
  - The reciprocity principle ... 21
  - Social proof ... 24
  - The principle of authority ... 27
  - The scarcity principle ... 30
  - Incentive law ... 33
- **CONVINCE BY ARGUING** ... 37
- **BOUNDARIES OF PERSUASION AND ARGUING** ... 41
- **DEFINITION OF NEGOTIATION** ... 44
  - Reasons to negotiate ... 47
  - Reasons to plan the negotiation ... 50
- **LEADERSHIP AND CHARISMA** ... 52
- **THE MAIN STYLES OF NEGOTIATION** ... 60
- **INTERESTS AND GOALS IN THE NEGOTIATION** ... 68
  - Classification and assessment of the objectives ... 72
  - Change of objectives ... 72
- **THE PROPOSAL** ... 74
- **RULES OF NEGOTIATION** ... 82
- **STAGES AND TECHNIQUES OF** ... 88
- **MISTAKES IN NEGOTIATION** ... 95
- **CONCLUSIONS** ... 101

Negotiate Like a Boss

Persuasion skills and negotiation techniques

Steven T. Walker

Galatea Editions

INTRODUCTION

What can I do to achieve everything I want? This is a question that we usually ask ourselves and it's based on the urgency of fulfilling our needs, our hopes, and simply, being happy.

The answer to this is: work hard so you can achieve it! Things don't fall from the sky, and it must be ourselves who seek to make that change that we need so that our goals are fulfilled.

The detail is that most times, the decisions we need to take to make those necessary changes happen, aren't only up to us, they also depend on the decisions other people make, and that's when the task gets a little complicated.

We're social beings by nature, we need to coexist with others so that we achieve things, we don't have the ability to be completely self-sufficient. That is why, through time, we have grouped in small, medium or large communities.

The interaction with the people who surround us causes on a daily basis not one, but several situations in which we must be prepared to persuade or negotiate. It's something as elemental as breathing, we need to do it even in the most basic things of everyday life; for instance, when a marriage talks to decide at what time they'll each rise the following morning: one wants to do it at 7:00 a. m., but the other one fathers it's at 8:00 a. m., and they both have to leave in the same vehicle. Complicated, right?

These aren't only routine situations, but on a larger scale they can set the course of our lives: like negotiating to accept a new and better job in a different town, or the choice to coexist with another person for the rest of your life. These are determinant actions that set a before and after, and if they're not handled correctly, can mean a setback and huge headache in the future.

With this book I want to show you which are the basic techniques that will help you persuade and negotiate with other people in a fool-proof way; if you follow this recipe, nothing can go wrong!

And that's what it's about, learning all the elemental stuff that you need to become an excellent negotiator, so that you can, without attacking or harming others, achieve everything you set your mind to and what every human hope for: accomplishing success and being happy!

In these lines I leave you strategies, anecdotes and all the basic stuff you need to know to become a skillful negotiator, a person who is willing and committed to achieving all of their goals.

We've always thought that this is a skill that is born with people, we think it's luck, charisma, but it really isn't that way. The ability to negotiate and persuade is something you can develop, in an easy or difficult way, you choose the path. I hereby provide you with the easy road, learning through reading; a completely different method from learning by trial and error, making over and over mistake after mistake, which is really frustrating and tiring.

The goals we set for ourselves, in one way or another, are always bound to our emotions. We must be disciplined to be able to control ourselves and skillful to lead others into our terrain and reach agreements that benefit both parties, but mainly you.

What happens then, when other people don't want the same as I do? That's where the problem lies and it's something completely normal: you're not the center of the world, surely, there will be others trying to accomplish what they want. When this happens, it's absolutely necessary to negotiate with others.

In this stage, it's necessary to be very intelligent,

though it's not the same intelligent with which you get the best grades in school, it's about that one you develop interacting with others and analyzing the situations that come up on a daily basis.

All that I offer you in this book is oriented to the development of that ability of persuasion and negotiation that every leader must have, to learn how to control yourself and also learn how to dominate situations without others realizing that in the end they'll act to your advantage.

You must be clear in what you're striving for, do you want to persuade or do you want to negotiate? Both actions are very different from each other: in negotiations you reach a settlement in which both parts have given something up as a measure of offer; on the other hand, in persuasion you influence someone else to modify their way of thinking, their beliefs and getting them to adopt your own as valuable.

To accomplish what you need it's important to know each in depth, which are their boundaries, the psychological laws persuasion is based on, negotiation styles, stages and techniques you can use in every case, among others.

Don't risk making rushed decisions, without assessing first the scenario and the consequences you'll face if you face it in that way, because surely the outcome won't be the best. It's necessary that your brain responds to these situations in an intelligent way, and for that, you must train it.

Observing the situation, identifying the possible risks, assessing the effects, processing the information and act according to them is the wisest thing you can do before taking any decision which will be determinant for your life. Though these techniques are applicable to everyday situations, it's also true that you shouldn't take anything that's associated to future-defining moments lightly.

It's fundamental that a good communication and disposition exists to mediate and reach agreements. It's important to know when to give in and when not to, because, as it's often said, "you can't win every time"; and when it's your turn to lose, then you have to fight to lose as least as possible.

Let's see, then, which are the infallible persuasion and negotiation techniques that will lead you, without a doubt, through a path of successes both in your personal and professional life.

CHAPTER 1.
ABOUT PERSUASION

We understand by rhetoric the faculty to take into account what is appropriate in each case to convince.

(Aristotle, ***Rhetoric***, **1355b, 25-26**)

What is persuasion?

Persuasion is the ability we have to influence others so that they do what we want, or believe in what we believe in. It is, fundamentally, the use of strategies in arguments to achieve a change of paradigms in a person in a way that they see things from our point of view.

It's necessary to take into account that persuading isn't the same as manipulating. When you manipulate, you change someone's behavior, based on threats, and loathsome attitudes, so that this person acts according to your benefit, regardless of how you might be affected.

In persuasion the method is completely different, you act in the right way, only trying to make the other person adopt your ideas as valuable because you're convinced that it's the best for both for them, or for the group, or even that specific person.

Many times, we see as other people solve situations in their lives in a rushed way, and we, from a calmer point of view, can see how things could be so much better. Our work then starts when we try to make the other person see what they're doing and how they can improve it; that's a way of persuading.

Another difference between manipulation and persuasion is the duration of the act itself. When you manipulate, you do it in a very specific way, since it's very likely that the other person notices your intentions at some point. However, when persuading, the goal is that the other person can see that your ideas are beneficial so they can adopt them as their own, resulting in a benefit and change of belief that can last for a long time.

You must consider that if you wish to establish a long-term relationship with the other party, the most recommended thing to do is to persuade, get close to that person; that will also guarantee you that said relationship will be based on wellbeing, truth, and the strong conviction to stay connected to it for a long period of time.

We must also differentiate persuasion from dissuasion. When we dissuade someone, we do it regardless of whether they'll believe or not in our idea at the end, the important thing is that the change in their thoughts happen, but not that they adopt it as truth. Persuasion is more emotional in that sense. At this point it is important that the person does things with the conviction that it's the right thing to do, because it's logical and because, in addition, it's a provable position.

To be able to persuade someone, you rely on the disposition that person has of listening to you, to be receptive enough to analyze and understand what you're saying. So, it's necessary that you have a certain degree of emotional intelligence so you can handle the situation and realize if your message is being received or not by the other person in the way you want.

To persuade someone you must become a good observant, based on their behavior, their attitude, to be able to approach them with your arguments without running the risk of being rejected. These explanations must be well based with a coherent and logical speech which forcefully accompanies the idea you're trying to express. So, part of your success in persuasion also depends on you being a good speaker, on being able to express yourself in a clear away to capture your listener.

In this way, persuasion has several elements which compose it:

✔ Emitter: In this case you would be the person who wishes to convince the other one to change their minds. You must make an effort to be honest and specially, believable.

✔ Receiver: It's the person who will receive your message, who you will be persuading. Your likelihood of success and how hard this task might or might not be, will depend on how emotionally and intellectually intelligent the person is.

I'd like to add that the level of intelligence in a person is not a determining factor to state that they can't be influenced. If they have deficiencies in the emotional part, you'll be able to persuade them anyway. The thing about intelligent people is that they can have more arguments to counter rest your idea, and that's when finding a way to change their beliefs, becomes tedious.

✔ Message: The type of message and the tone in which you project it are fundamental to persuade someone. First, the subject has to be of interest for the other person, or else, how would you manage to capture their attention? The second thing is that, according to the receiver's personality, you try to modify your speech in a way that the message reaches them effectively and can affect another deep-rooted thought.

✔ Way of transmitting the message: The way in which you transmit the message is one of the guarantees of success or failure in persuasion. You can persuade by being sympathetic, promoting reciprocity, wrapping people up in society's proper questions, and using other techniques that I'll explain in detail further on, in the following chapter of this book.

Keep in mind that in order to persuade someone, you

mustn't be direct or obvious, since this can upset the person; you must learn to be subtle, discreet, in such a way that by the end, the person believes that it was their own thinking ability and reasoning about things which led them to change, whether it's a change in their behavior or in the way of thinking.

Persuasion must be an imperceptible art, a very intelligent way of making others take your ideas or adopt behaviors based on your beliefs. You must make the other person see things from your perspective and choose according to it, always trying, of course, that there is a win-win relationship that allows both to obtain benefits, or that at least, it allows the person to enjoy the positive things you're already enjoying.

CHAPTER 2
THE PSYCHOLOGICAL LAWS OF PERSUASION

It's very important for persuasion (…) the way in which the speaker presents themselves and the fact that it can be assumed that he has a certain attitude regarding the listeners, just like, the way they refer to them, the fact that it is accomplished that they also have a specific attitude towards the speaker.

(Aristotle, *Rhetoric*, 1377b, 25-29)

There are certain techniques, based mainly on the personality types and the emotional intelligence, which can help you make persuasion a hundred percent effective in a quicker, and more elaborate way, without making the other person feel threatened or forced to do something they don't really want to do.

These principles are based on the basic human being's psychology, and the fact of unravelling what makes us do things. Is it entirely our own criteria or do we get carried away by situations and feelings? Why yes, most times when we decide something it happens under a certain influence, and with these laws what I seek to teach you is to be the spark necessary to trigger the reaction.

Imagine, for a moment, a woman without a single drop of makeup on her face trying to sell lipstick: complete madness! I assure you'll never buy anything from them, and this is due to the fact that you can't sell others something you don't even use. It happens the same with ideas, it's necessary that you lead by example, with sympathy, and that according to the situation you decide which strategy to use to achieve your purpose.

Knowing the different ways in which you can persuade a person will open up a wide spectrum of opportunities to our eyes. We can use one or several, depending on the situation, but normally, according to your personality, there will always be one that stands out from the rest. This will be your particular way of doing things.

The laws I introduce to you up next are recognized and put into practice by the best negotiators in the world, they are, definitely, a toolbox you should keep in your repertoire of strategies to persuade other people.

Persuasion by sympathy

It's completely normal that when someone close to us asks for something, we at least have, at first, the willingness of assessing if we reply to their request in a positive or negative way. This doesn't happen with strangers because we'll always be more careful and have reservations about them. So, it's all about the sympathy we can cause on the person that we're trying to persuade.

This persuasion technique has, metaphorically speaking, a sharp, two-headed spear: the first is affinity and the second is praise. Applying both is a guarantee of success to achieve what you set your mind to.

Did you know that *marketing* and sales studies have proven that when you establish some sort of affinity and praise between the parties, it's much easier and certain that you'll be able to persuade them into buying the product, even putting this above the product's characteristics or whether they truly need it?

Meaning, that "bond" that's somehow established between the salesman and the buyers facilitates the sell, and all of this, simply because there's a certain level of closeness, of resemblance between the parties, and also the salesman always uses as a strategy, sweetening the other person up a little bit, and this they do, generally, by praising them.

This strategy is similarly applied in the areas of interpersonal relationships and business.

To persuade a person using sympathy, it's necessary to cause liking or everything that could promote affinity, a feeling that literally brings two people close together, and in some way familiarizes them.

So, it's very important that if you're going to persuade someone, you try to know what their tastes and interests are, in a way that you can approach them through the subject and you can manage to initially establish a relationship based on the affinity between you both. It's far easier that a person gives into your goals when there's a certain companionship, an empathetic relationship, when they simply like you; because they will feel more trusting and have less fear of being vulnerable or harmed; you must try to earn their trust in any way.

The other point of the spear is praise. Who doesn't feel good with a person that always brings up what your best qualities are? We all feel good! Sure, you must be very intelligent, because this should be done in a very subtle way. The idea is not to be exaggerated about it because what you seek to achieve is the other person's sympathy, not the opposite.

I know sometimes it can be difficult, especially when the other person isn't open and their qualities aren't the best, but you must be very observant and try to identify in them an aspect that, for you, is sincerely worthy of praise. As possible, like added value, it would be good that it's also something you have in common, because you'd be stumping inside the other person's terrain with their own shoes.

Achieving to persuade someone from sympathy comes from the fact that we tend to think that if a person who appreciates us, admires us, recommends us something, they'll undoubtedly will be doing it in good faith, with good intentions, because they want to help us; and in this way we'll agree because to us, it'll be convenient.

That's why, when we're compatible, what happens deep down is that we trust more in each other, it's a part of what establishes relationships with our loved ones, with our couple, with our friends, or with good business partners and work companions.

If you want to achieve sympathy in others it's necessary that you're measured, sincere, nonjudgmental, very educated and empathic, and also give them a certain level of importance.

Yes, the importance and attention that we give to the other person is essential to get their sympathy. Paying a lot of attention when they're talking and try to always bring up subjects related to their strengths, make them feel good and using sincere flattery is the best tactic so that this person pays attention to you and also considers carrying out something you want.

When you want to persuade through sympathy someone that you think is wrong, try not to always cut to the chase, making a direct commentary on their mistake, since this, instead of being positive, will create a clash between the both of you. Remember that, in that moment, that person is convinced that they're right.

The best thing you can do is promote situations or conversations in which, by themselves, that person can identify their mistake. It must be something imperceptible, in a way that they feel like they're realizing it by themselves and giving them the chance to think of their mistake and fix it. At this point, you must be supportive and take advantage and expose your idea, always starting off from the fact that making mistakes is a human thing, it has happened to you as well, and that there's nothing wrong with correcting those mistakes and moving on.

Being sympathetic to persuade is one of the best tools you can use, especially when it comes to leading groups of people. You must earn the trust of the team and do as you can to create a certain leadership so they can see you as a role model, a trustful person to which they can go to when something goes wrong, or an ally to chase common goals.

To persuade using sympathy you must be able to start, and keep a good conversation with the other person. Try to talk to them like you're friends from a long time ago, to give them a comfort, pleasant, and warm feeling.

Try to always be a fun person, to be in a good mood, have a sense of humor, without becoming the buffoon of the room; this will allow you to approach others in a better way and you will have at your disposal, firsthand, the information you need from them to know their interests and personal likings. Additionally, and according to this, if there is something you can share with them, whether it's an activity, information, or simply a good conversation and a cup of coffee, I'll assure you that they'll help you settle the ground towards persuasion.

The reciprocity principle

Let's start by understanding what it means to be reciprocal: associated with an exchange action in which you seek to give and receive in the same measure. As people commonly say "give what you want to receive", that's the predisposition we all must have to treat others just like they treat us.

When we're thoughtful with other people, what we get from them is, generally, at least a thankful gesture. Of course, this is not an exact rule, there are people who don't appreciate details or other people's attention, but in the great majority of folks, it generates a certain level of acknowledgement and what is produced as a consequence is a retribution.

Applying the law of reciprocity to persuade can bring you positive results, to start, the fundamental thing is that your collaborator will have a positive attitude towards you, and this is essential to give you the opportunity of being heard and to make yourself a place in their thoughts or opinions.

A way to make others be reciprocal is by setting the example. If you're the first to expose yourself and demonstrate that your idea is valid and applicable to the point of testing it yourself, others will feel a greater confidence in doing the same, also showing you the level of commitment to your goals.

In a way, when we give others part of our knowledge or we share situations to reach a certain goal together, the other person will feel related to you, even indebted for having trusting them and making them a part of the process. They'll feel useful and appreciated, and this will bring as a consequence a great disposition to help you.

Situations in general always behave as a boomerang, this is left clear in the anecdote I will share with you next.

Once upon a time there was a farmer that, walking through a prairie, heard in the distance a young boy's cries who, desperate, called out for help. He had slipped and fallen on a lake and he didn't know how to swim, so without giving it further thought, the farmer jumped in the water to help him out. The young boy, still frightened, thanked the farmer and then, still afraid, went home. When he got there and told his father what had happened, he looked up where the farmer lived and went up to his house and, as a thankful gesture he offered to pay for his son's education, including university.

The farmer's son turned out to be Alexander Fleming, who, after graduating as a doctor, invented penicillin, with which he saved the young man's life who his father saw drowning years before, evidently not so young anymore, since he had contracted pneumonia.

The moral of this story is that one hand washes the other and that you don't know when you'll be in need of the other person: life is truly a boomerang.

Notice how a simple event, apparently isolated, had such forceful consequences that had repercussions on all of mankind. Can you imagine what would've happened to us if penicillin hadn't been invented? Surely, our situation would be completely different.

This anecdote shows how, when we do something, this will always bring an associated reaction with it. The famous "consequence of your actions" that we're all exposed to when we make decisions.

When persuading, try to always do it by seeking to get the reaction you're looking for. For instance, if you want a person to provide you with information about something, start off by sharing your information with them. By doing so, you'll create more trust, liking and also a feeling of returning the favor you're doing them.

When you persuade from reciprocity, in a way, the person feels obliged to repay you something due to the attitude you've had with them, so everything comes from what you're willing to give to achieve that the other person is perceptive and grateful to you.

Has it ever happened to you that you get to a place and a stranger smiles at you as a sign to wish you a good day? What is your reaction? Probably, smiling back, unless you're having a bad day. The case is that, regularly, we give others what we receive from them, and this makes persuasion more effective.

To illustrate a little bit better what you can achieve with reciprocity, think about when you go to the supermarket and you find a gentle and educated person who, with much kindness and a smile, invites you to try out a new product. What do you do? The most likely thing is that you agree to it, since it will make you feel remorse to have been treated so nicely and deny their request.

The same thing happens in those situations which present themselves to us on a daily basis. If someone is kind to you and asks you to do something, you'll hardly refuse their request. It's very unlikely that you won't want to m, at least, try to please them, since it's a matter of courtesy, of socializing, and of not exposing yourself in the future to, for not having replied positively to something, being a victim of your own judgement, but in a negative way.

Social proof

Human beings are, by nature, social beings, we are obligated to interact with each other for our survival. It's impossible that we can live isolated from the rest of the world, in everything, in one way or another, we're structured into groups to be able to fulfill our physical and emotional demands.

Our way of thinking, feeling or acting is always influenced by our surroundings, not only the physical one, but also by the people who surround us.

We tend to follow a social pattern. If we feel related to the causes that move others, we'll probably associate them to complement them and benefit from them. It's a way to feel like a part of the group, to be socially accepted.

When you persuade taking into account social norms, there's a high chance of success, because the person will see reflected in the group, or in others, what they want for themselves, they'll understand the point and feel related to it, getting them to agree to our requests. In a wat, seeing several people in the same situation will give the persuaded person confidence and their disposition to join and follow the guidelines the group dictates will be greater

The best example of this is when you walk by a restaurant and you see a lot of people in it, even waiting outside for others to leave so they can have a place. What's the first thing you think about? That they have really good food! And this will give you more security if you choose to eat at this place. This is a way of persuading the customers so they walk in the place and try their dishes, letting them see how many people go to the restaurant and, in some cases, they advertise using the diners' opinions, giving their testimony about their experience there.

For anthropological reasons, we act like we're part of a pack, like that was necessary to be able to survive inside the society we belong to. It's nearly impossible that we see others act in a way, see positive results, and not want to try it out.

So, when you try to persuade someone and you use the social example as foundation to orchestrate your strategy, it's very improbable that things don't go the way you want them to. There are many people who base their decision making on others' experiences, because they're too afraid to venture into something completely new that they don't know how it'll go.

Now, it's important that you're careful with the "being sociable" subject. You don't always want to be part of the flock, sometimes it's better to follow your gut and show others that changes can be much more productive, especially for our interests. Then, when persuading, always do it taking into account that the probability of success in relation to the benefits obtained is the highest, because, aside from making persuasion effective, it'll make you win credibility and admiration: two powerful weapons when it comes to influencing others.

This persuasion technique is based on the human beings' necessity of adapting, integrating and not feeling out of place inside their own environment. Many times, we imitate others, and precisely this is what is being taken advantage of in this form of persuasion.

The approval and practice ideas adopted by the masses give us the argument credibility, trust ability; using an idea that's framed by this aspect gives you a warrant of success, that you'll achieve what you're looking for.

A strategy that works very skillfully when it comes to applying this technique, is persuading the person to follow someone else's behavior, like a pattern, just for the fact that it's socially accepted. For instance, have you ever been in a study group and bought something to eat that you didn't like, just to "fit in" with the person you ate it with, without saying anything? Or has it ever happened to you that you bought or collaborated in something that wasn't of your liking, but since other known people were doing it, you decided to join in? Probably, the answer is yes, and this is due to the fact that, when facing the need of belonging to a social group, we all react in a positive way towards it.

This proves that it's understandable that the more people adjust or adapt to an idea or behavior, the easier it will be to make others, by association, become a part of it, and take it for themselves as a lifestyle, as a belief.

Your role when persuading someone using social proof is to show them that others have already put into practice or adopted your idea, and make them see the results it has caused, so that they feel calm when doing the same thing, as we usually think, if it works for them, why wouldn't it work for me?

This is considered to be social informative influence, a phenomenon that makes people condition their behavior and thoughts based on the behavior that other people have in the situation.

With the impact of social media and web selling platforms it's very common that we try to make our shopping this way since it's more comfortable and simpler, besides the fact that we are able to easily see the different options. Most of the times, aside from the necessity itself that we have for the product, we always look for information about the seller's qualification to know how trustable they are. This is a marketing strategy based on social proof.

When you use this technique, always try to tell anecdotes about other people who have put your idea into motion, how they've been doing; if you can even say the names of known people, it would be a lot better. This will give your speech a greater weight and you'll manage to put the other person in your favor.

The principle of authority

Using the principle of authority to persuade is a more elaborate work. The first thing you must do is demonstrate your knowledge about the subject with which you want to influence the other person, that way, they will feel like they're really taking a step on steady ground because an expert illustrated them about the subject.

Multiple studies have shown that the simple fact of putting on display the academic learning, preparation or judgement about a subject, really improves the receptivity others have when the information comes from a person who truly knows what they're talking about.

Work hard to make your knowledge known, but do it in an imperceptible way, within the conversations you have with the other person, slowly, so that they don't think that you're trying to brag over your achievements. It helps a lot if you're promoting some kind of social bond between the two of you, because the person will feel more confident, more relaxed.

There are many cases in which, to make a negotiation some informal meetings are previously done, dinner, lunch, coffee; dinner, lunch, a coffee; this with the endgame that all people involved can spend time together and, in a way, promote what we've already discussed about affinity and sympathy. In said meeting you can take advantage and tell your experiences related to the subject, or to expose your academic achievements, without bragging, but in a subtle way within the conversation that is happening.

Now, you don't always get the necessary time for these types of meetings, so you must take advantage of a previous conversation to the appointment so you can make clear the control you have about the subject. This will help give your speech the importance and respect it deserves as soon as you choose to present your arguments to persuade the other person to take part in your ideas.

In the family and social areas, it happens the same, every time we say something, it's more believable if we have some sort of experience in it, something similar to the example I mentioned earlier about makeup. How do you make another woman wear it if the saleswoman doesn't use it? This makes it clear that she's not a person who's an expert in the subject and that she's simply trying to make you buy the product without actually caring if it's going to be good on your skin, if you'll manage to hide some perfections or just improve your features. In this case, the most likely thing to happen is that persuasion won't work.

This persuasion technique is associated with the term authority, which is defined as: "Prestige and credit given to a person or institution for their legitimacy or their quality and competence in any matter". Meaning, it's the faculty that gives you the right and power to give your opinion or make a decision about something.

Then, you must know which are the aspects that can give you some sort of authority over someone or something to be able to put into motion your persuasion plan. Which things can cause this?

- **The place:** You must find a place that gives strength and a foundation to your arguments when exposing them, this will cause a greater impact in the receiver.
- **Lesser responsibility:** Try to always bring together several people with the same idea. In a way, they'll each feel bad if things don't go out as expected, they'll have less responsibility because there are people following the same criteria.
- **Work on your integrity:** To be able to generate authority on other people, it's necessary that you're an upright person, with a high value standard in the eyes of

everybody else.
- **Watch your presence:** When you dress and tidy up properly for the occasion, this gives your speech a better presence and, therefore, a better reach.
- **Stay close:** Every time you wish to exert your authority on others it will be necessary that you're near them, the effect is not the same when sending an email, calling their phone, than being present. This will allow you to monitor everything firsthand, realizing if one or several people in the group were not paying attention to what you've been trying to influence on them and thus, causing others to do so too.

Authority is also associated to the role you play. For instance, in the family area, you can't persuade your brother to do something because he sees you as an equal, unless you've done some things that make you worthy of his respect and admiration.

To achieve that your speech has a voice of command, the other person must be a subordinate, so in this case you'll have to be one of the parents to get all the necessary total support.

This point is a bit algid because authority must come not only with a position within the social circle, you should also be empathetic, coherent, compromised and respectful, fundamental values to get the other person to tend to your ideas and adopt them.

To close up this point and make clear what it means to persuade using the principle of authority, I leave you the following case.

There are many patients that when left in therapy, in the hands of the hospital's staff, abandon the therapy because they feel like they're not people technically capable of guiding them, that they're not proper doctors and the results won't be effective. Truly, many times the doctor isn't a specialist in therapy itself, but they do a follow-up of the pathology the patient presents. Those who are in charge of the recovery are others, who know the exercises and the ways in which you must do them in depth.

Even if you don't believe so, it's actually effective to hang people's degrees and merits on the walls of the hospitals. Do you know why? Because if you go to a place to be cared for by someone and you realize that the person is certified to do so, it'll give you a greater confidence and you'll know that you're putting your recovery in expert and qualified hands. You feel like that person has a certain authority to do what they're doing.

The scarcity principle

The scarcity principle emphasizes the short availability of something, whether it's a resource, time or any other associated thing, in order to influence the person, we want to convince to do or buy something, whether it's an item or an idea.

Has it ever happened to you that when someone tells you that something is running out you start panicking and you want to go out and buy it right away? Well, it happens the same when we want to persuade someone: the mere thought that something might not be available later or that it'll simply be a long time before you have that opportunity again, makes the person react and see themselves practically forced to make a quick decision, which gives you the power to persuade them much more easily.

In a way, you use in this persuasion technique the language of loss, you put the other person in the perspective of seeing themselves in the situation of losing or not having something, and this automatically influences their ability to make decisions.

It also has something to do with the law of offer and demand. Generally, we associate the things that have a limited stock as "valuable". If there's something in abundance on the market, we think that it's because it has nothing good to offer and that's why we don't take it.

Without a doubt, when something is scarce, its value rises.

Another thing that is important is expectation. When we get information or something in a measured way, we keep the other part interested in knowing what else there is, in thinking what it would be like to have more, what outcomes it would have. This creates a very particular attention on the subject and the influence achieved will be greater, because the other person is anxious to learn more about what it is that you can potentially give them.

There is another aspect within the scarcity principle called the "patrimony effect". Refers to the fact that we usually convince ourselves that those things that belong to us have a greater value than any other. Suddenly we can acquire something much better at a very good price or even for free, as is the case of the knowledge that another person can provide us with. The thing is we value those things more, simply because they belong to us already. The feeling of loss that we experience for not having something that we've already had is greater, more difficult to overcome.

When we want to persuade someone using the scarcity law, it's necessary that we take certain things into account, which makes it so effective:

- Generally, people often want what others can't have, it's the way to feel special.
- We also tend to want what others want, leaning to the healthy competition that many times we take on to win something, to prove to others or simply to ourselves that we can achieve it. The motivational powers of competition are impressive because you require a greater effort to achieve and keep something, because you feel like others are also on the lookout.
- In a way, scarcity generates publicity, the fact of not having things at hand, and even having to wait for them at times.
- The scarcity principle provides you with the op-

portunity to disaggregate a little about who is truly interested in your idea, and who will be an easy target when the time for persuasion comes. They're the ones who will make a greater effort to be attentive to the situation.

The context in which we establish our ideas, as much as the meaning that they have to us are important. How can we convince anyone of something if we don't place them in the right setting? This is also vital when we speak of scarcity and persuasion.

The scarcity principle directly attacks the bad habit that we have of procrastinating: we're always delaying things, saving them for later, postponing them, we don't realize that we're wasting opportunities. We love waiting for things to turn difficult and more attractive to others, or even owned by others, to want to have them. Use this so that, in that very moment, you sell your idea, persuade someone to acquire a product or simply make a person do what you want.

Let's see the following story to understand a little bit more about how it works.

Once Upon a Time A well-dressed man arrived in town, he settled in the only Hotel there was and he put a notice in the only page of the local newspaper. He was willing to buy every monkey that was brought to him for 10 pesos. The peasants, knowing that the forest was filled with monkeys, went running to hunt them.

The man bought, as he had promised in the notice, the hundreds of monkeys that were brought to him at the settled price. But, when there were very few monkeys left in the forest and it was difficult to hunt them, the peasants lost interest. Then, the man offered 15 pesos for each one, and the peasants ran back to the forest.

There were less and less monkeys each time and the man raised his offer to 20 pesos. The peasants went back into the forest, hunted the very few monkeys that were left until it was almost impossible to find one. At this point, the man offered 50 pesos for each. But, as he had business to run in the city, he would leave his helper be-

hind, who approached the peasants by telling them: "Look at this cage filled with hundreds of monkeys that my boss bought for his collection. Now that he's gone, I'll sell them to you at 30 pesos each, when my boss returns from the city you'll sell them to him at 50 pesos each".

The peasants put together all of their savings and bought the hundreds of monkeys that were in the big cage and waited for the boss's return. From that day forward, they never saw the boss nor the helper again. All they saw was the cage filled with monkeys that they bought with their lifetime savings. This is how the bubbles in the stock market are formed with dire consequences for whole nations.[1]

Incentive law

We all act spurred by the need of something, by the motivation of achieving our own goals or making a positive change in others. To do this we attend to social exchange, to bonding with other people to establish a win-win relationship from which both parties are benefitted.

When we establish relationships in which the cost, whether it's material or sentimental, is greater than the benefit we're getting, that's when the choice of ending the relationship is taken.

When we persuade using an incentive, it's because we're offering the other person, in return of accepting our ideas, an associated benefit; we stimulate them to our favor so we can get what we want.

When I speak of an incentive it doesn't necessarily mean money, it can be anything else that the person considers to be "valuable", something that is positive for them to obtain because it brings them personal satisfaction. For instance, in the professional area, it's not

---

[1] Llantada, A. *The black book of persuasion*, pages. 49-50.

enough to motivate an employee with a bonus. If you want to really persuade them into doing the work in the time and quality that you require, it's important that you also mention their achievements, credit them for their involvement in reaching the goal.

Incentives have to match the person you persuade, not everyone has the same interests and, therefore, not everyone wants the same things. What can be amazing to me, might not even seem practical to you or be of your liking, so this is the main reason why when giving Awards there's always several options, trying to tend to the entire market.

It happens the same when in persuading someone, you have to properly adjust that the motivation you offer is actually attractive for the person or the group. If you offer something that isn't of their interest, they'll simply won't pay much attention to you.

All human beings act by stimulus, in a rational way, we assess and think everything under the logic and the consequences that a certain situation may bring to us. I ask you; would you respond positively to something that isn't productive or functional to you? Absolutely not! You wouldn't even waste your time on it, because you simply wouldn't care.

A skillful strategy to incentivize others is to let them try some of the sweetness of the success they'll get if they achieve the goal or follow the ideas you propose. Letting them savor the prize first and then taking it away is a way of capturing their attention and motivating them to want to have it again. Next up, I'll illustrate this with an example.

During the Olympic Games a marathon was made, the winner was a runner who was practically immediately disqualified and his prize was withdrawn.

Why was he disqualified? At first, it was a misunderstanding: the runner felt ill in the middle of the race and he asked someone who passed by in their car to give them a ride to the stadium so he could get his things.

When he arrived, he felt better, and the crowd started to cheer on him, thinking that he had already come back and he would be the first person to cross the finish line, and he, jokingly, decided to run towards it. It was such the public's enthusiasm that the athlete got carried away and he didn't say how he had gotten there, but eventually they noticed and took away his prize.

What happened next? The following year, this runner prepared himself and won the marathon, since he felt so much shame and wanted to live the experience in an honest way, this worked as motivation for him to win the prize

The story is, definitely, a clear demonstration of what motivation can cause, so that a person chases the finish line, works hard and puts their focus in all of their efforts and achieves that which, at some point, had in their hands and lost. It's something that is also associated with the scarcity principle, something we discussed in the previous point.

But we must know how to administer incentives. We can't completely give everything away from the beginning because then, what would you have left to persuade people with? I think not much. Imagine you are at home with your children and you offer them a cookie as a reward for being good; the problem lies in offering the full jar of cookies. What would you offer then? You wouldn't really have nothing.

Another thing is that incentives must vary, adapt to the needs and the new tendencies that come up. For instance, if you want someone to buy a raffle ticket and you offer a vintage TV, from the 90s, obviously, it won't be attractive to anyone. You must offer a last-generation TV so that the purchase of the ticket becomes attractive for potential customers.

Sometimes, we think that incentivizing someone is easy, you offer something and that's it. But actually, it's not that way. If you look beyond, it's necessary to pay a lot of attention to detail and have a lot of determination and objectivity to focus your goal on the behavior of that person, so that then, once they've already achieved it, they don't feel like you've scammed them to try and accomplish your purpose.

When motivating someone to persuade them, keep in mind the following:

o   Make sure that the motivation is your initiative, but that the other person is the one to feed it. That way, it'll feel to them like it's their own accomplishments and it will be much more gratifying.

o   Try to delete the limits the person has set for themselves, let them know that they're more able to achieve even more than what they think.

o   Motivate through example, you can't ask someone to do something if you don't practice it. Increase your reputation and a healthy ego to do so.

o   Make sure you give recognition to the other person and they achieve the established goal. The reward is gratification, but the recognition is on a superior level in our emotions.

CHAPTER 3
CONVINCE BY ARGUING

Also, an appropriate way of speaking makes the matter believable, since the soul of the listener wrongly deduces that the speaker is telling the truth because they do so in such circumstances, in a way that they believe, even if it's not right, that everything is just as they say, and the listener always sympathizes with the speaker who talks with passion, even if they say nonsense. That's why many people impress the listeners by simply speaking loudly.

(Aristotle, *Rhetoric*, 1408a, 16-25)

We live in a society in which we all have different thoughts. We can agree with some people in our convictions or beliefs, but it's impossible that we all think the same way; we would be, in every case, a species of robots programmed under the same schemes. Nothing further away from the truth.

When our ideas differ from everyone else's, many times we need, in a way, to convince them these aren't right or perhaps they're not the best. How many times has it happened that we're the ones who are wrong, but we're still convinced that we own the truth, we still fill ourselves with arguments to try and persuade the other person about what we think.

For this reason, to influence others and make them change their convictions, we fill ourselves with arguments, which are the result of the reasoning of an idea that is trying to be proven to someone, to show that our proposal is valuable. What we do is try to convince the other person, with proof, if possible, that they're wrong;

or exposing to them very clearly our way of thinking, which must be logical and cohesive to achieve a change in the other person

It's not an easy task, since the goal isn't simply to express ourselves, it's a deep change in thought, so we must, in the strict sense, argue to convince.

When we are in a conversation with someone, exposing our ideas, there are ways to realize that they're being receptive to the speech or not. If you observe their body language and the way they reply to you, you can know if you're on the right track.

When this interaction happens, there are two levels which are equally affected and for which it's difficult to manage the persuasion. Each one in its own way: the first one is the other person, who walks in the dilemma of having to assess their own opinions and the consequences of what it means to change them, sometimes for good, but if the person is still closed off, they won't manage to see it so easily; on the second level there's you... it's not easy to argue! Even though you're right, there's always an obstacle in trying to convince the other person, and it is you who must keep in mind a strategy with the points that you think can make a dent in their way of thinking, accompanied of course, by a strong and rooted speech that shows the person your conviction for the idea you proposing.

Arguing implies giving reasons to the other person so they make a change of paradigm, adopting our way of thinking. To do so, it's not necessary to use any tricks, threats or manipulation. Every time you try to negotiate with someone you're supposed to do so with the best intentions, exposing rational causes why they should change the way they've been thinking until now and persuading them to make a change out of their free will, without any type of coercion used to accomplish this.

When arguing, the important thing is not being liked by the other person. It obviously helps but the essential thing is that our points are so unobjectionable that the other person can't defend themselves in the face of our position. For this, you don't have to be the most outgoing or competent person when speaking, a shy person can accomplish this as well. The only thing you need is to find the exact ways in which you can capture their attention and lay strong arguments to prove your point of view and make the other person reflect about it.

Don't think that because you're shy you won't be able to make it, imagine all the people that have speech problems. The stutterers, for a start, you might not believe it, but they can get to be efficient salesmen. The important thing isn't how we look, or if we have gifts or incentives to persuade the other person, what's really important is what we say and the way in which we say it. You can give thousands of gifts to a person and keep them wrapped up in your gallantry, but if your arguments and your speech are inappropriate, you're still not going to get anything from them.

We all have the ability to argue and convince someone else regardless of our social condition or the way in which we unfold. Do some of us have more tools or advantages than others? Yes, I'm not going to lie to you. But you must not limit yourself to think that you can't make it, because the important thing is not a good lexicon or the oratory skills you have, what's truly worthwhile is what's being said.

If the information you have is good, surely your arguments will be heavy and, therefore, they will be legitimately oriented to become a weapon from which no one can escape.

We have three ways of communicating things: informing, convincing or expressing. What's the difference between each one of them? If what you want is to give a description of the situation without getting involved, then you're oriented to informing; if, on the contrary, aside from the description you want to expose the feelings and emotions that this causes in you, undoubtedly the choice is to express.

Now, convincing is something else, because it's about involving both, information and expression, and turning them into a solid argument to motivate someone to make a change of mind. Generally, these are things that are intangible. If it weren't that way, we wouldn't have to convince anyone about them, they'll be right there, people will be able to see them. But when it's not like this, it's necessary to turn to arguments.

Each person has an opinion of things, so goes the saying "each head is a world of its own"; and each and every one of those opinions are totally arguable.

Opinions can be generated by a conflict of interests, professional situations, social debates, judicial discussions, couple or familial relationships, or due to exchange situations in the sales and advertising markets.

As I said at the beginning, not everyone thinks the same, but it's absolutely necessary that, in some cases, we take choices in common. And for this, we must at least moderately agree. This is when it's fundamental that each party exposes their ideas or arguments and they can be assessed in conjunction to reach an agreement.

Here comes into play the equality principle: to make this negotiation more viable you must be willing not only to expose your ideas, but also to the possibility of changing your mind, being open to possible change.

You must keep in mind that when you argue to convince, just like you have the opportunity to expose your ideas, the other person will have it too. This person is free to accept or reject your hypothesis, and to reply with other arguments that can finally make you change your mind and prove to you that their idea was much better. So, we must be rational and be open to change.

CHAPTER 4
BOUNDARIES OF PERSUASION AND ARGUING

The speaker must know the intentions of the other party with as much precision as a general knows its enemies.

(Quintilian, *Institutes of oratory*, XII, 1, 35)

A correct persuasion starts by capturing the discrepancy of thoughts in other people and avoiding, as much as possible, to be overconfident in the ability that we think we have to persuade.

It's necessary to design a coherent message to be able to perform an efficient persuasion. A mistake that is commonly made is wasting too much time in convincing the other person, instead of using more time to balance their abilities and competencies to discover what they want.

Our way of seeing and doing things isn't the only possible thing in the whole world. Every person does things in a different way, every person has their own way of thinking and acting in different situations that they go through. Persuasion can only work when there aren't facts, meaning, influencing to achieve a goal in a way that is reached through the action that the influenced person will perform, who at the same time will execute such action due to the clear intention that was presented to them.

In a negotiation, many mistakes are made because a variety of speech is used in which, through defenses and persuasive reasonings, it manages to convince us, with the intention of using them in the same way to convince others, being possible that it works out just like it doesn't.

Imagine yourself as a child (or your little one) not willing to eat your cauliflower. In such a case, your mother will appeal to persuasion to convince you to do so. It doesn't work. As much as she tells you that cauliflower is great for your health and for your eating habits, that it contains fibers, that you'll get super strong... It's useless! It's like talking to a wall. And they're very persuasive arguments, but to her, and not to you.

What should your mother do then? Negotiate. How? By asking herself: "What do I have that my child wants?". For example, you love chocolate ice cream. We can start negotiating. As the other method doesn't work, she tries this: "Honey, if you don't eat your cauliflower, I won't give you the delicious chocolate ice cream that I bought for you". We won't waste time adding reasons to defend our argument about the benefits of the cauliflower, but instead of convincing, you look for this change, meaning, you eat your vegetables and, in return, you win the ice cream that you love so much.

Besides, if she wants to gain power she can add, tactfully and sharply, a sanction. It works this way: "Honey, I have taken out the chocolate ice cream that you love so much from the fridge, but it's melting away because of the heat. Finish your dish of cauliflower and I'll give it to you for dessert". In this case, she will be showing you that the ice cream is melting away because of the heat (sanction) and she'll get you to, quickly, do what she wants (eat your cauliflower as soon as possible). Meaning, you negotiate because the persuasion phase has worn out without any results.

There are two types of negotiators in the cases in which persuasion doesn't always work:

a. They specialize in opposing everything, all of their sentences start with "it's just that". Generally, this type of person doesn't collaborate by coming up with solutions to the organization and they are known for having an unpleasant personality. It is called the "**disgus-**

ting" one.

b. Those who are fast and bold to find flaws in others and focus on the negative and what is wrong. Most of their arguments begin with "yes, but". These people are called the **"Yes, but'ers"**.

Before you try to negotiate, verify that your arguments are right and that they don't stop you from doing a proposal, considering that this is what makes a negotiation move forward. Sometimes, we want to convince and even impose our own reasons and thoughts, trying to prove that the wrong ones are the others because they don't share the same point of view.

An experienced negotiator sets as a goal to prepare an offer, and they don't waste time in providing resources to defend their argument.

CHAPTER 5
DEFINITION OF NEGOTIATION

Never will the speaker want to act unjustly.

(Plato, *Gorgias*, 460c)

To be able to understand the concept of negotiation in a clear way, you must first talk about its engine, "exchange", which is the face in which you grant something in exchange for something else.

This method, which has as a primary goal to fix some conflict, has two defined rules that the parties must be absolutely aware of without the intervention of any third party (once called, in the world of negotiation, the endogenous method):

- The first rule is based on the fact that **"negotiating is not to give in".** In a negotiation you seek to gain a benefit without the need of losing a favorable position. The expert negotiator in the area doesn't look to give in, but he sets exchange as a goal to achieve.
- The second golden rule is based on the fact that **"negotiating isn't convincing"**. Not about finding evidence or reasons to achieve an agreement and change your counterpart's way of thinking, or selling an idea through persuasion, negotiating is for sending arguments with which you reach an agreement or a solution for both of the parties' benefit.

"Negotiating is the activity in which two or more parties are involved when, despite having a conflict of interests, they also have a convenient mutual area where the differences can be worked out" (Japanese School of Negotiation).

Negotiation is born from the combination of instruments and models who seek to perfect a distinction between the negotiable processes.

The instruments for the resolution of a conflict are the tools or resources used as a means to reach an end. In negotiation, there are two types:

Compulsive instruments: They're the most used resources to affect the freedom of the process of decision-making in the same way in which you make an offer.

When using a coercive proposal, you seek to modify the result no matter if the proposal is attractive or not, the goal is to close a deal in the direction the negotiator wishes to.

An expert negotiator often uses this instrument with the goal of conquering an agreement. They do what's possible to dilate its use, but without completely ruling out its application. It doesn't mean that it has to be used, in fact, there are many successful negotiations that go down without applying this resource.

Mainly, you seek to reach an agreement without having to use resources, arguments and pressure, like coerced commitments, threats or any other mechanism which will bring tension to the negotiation or that it motivates both parties to use compulsive instruments.

Non compulsive instruments: Contrary to the previous one, in this type, there is freedom of reasoning without being reduced to a single viable option, trying, through the use of reasons and the arguments to reach the disposition of achieving agreeable terms without having to use resources that will direct the behavior to a single negotiation line. It is only intended to accomplish a change in behavior in spite of a group of reasons.

A negotiation based on the exchange of arguments is

better than a negotiation that lacks any argumentative activity.

Non compulsive instruments basically depend on the quality of the negotiation and not on the model of compromise of said negotiation

The ways to solve a conflict involve a group of scenarios and the way in which a conflict or situation might end up.

In a negotiation there are four ways of solving a conflict:

- **Imposition:** it's about the supremacy of the benefits from one of the parties in comparison to the other one, but still not giving up their own thoughts. The ideal thing in a negotiation is to be open to decline some of our advantages so we can reach an agreement in which the other person also gives up some of their interests. Which doesn't happen in this case because one of the actors of the conflict achieves complete success of their goals above their counterpart's goals.
- **The retreat:** In a negotiation you can talk about a retreat when one of the parties that seek the settlement abandons the process and, automatically, the other party's goals prevail. Meaning, one of the actors decides to desist from the confrontation and protection of their goals.
- **The conversion:** This scenario has a particularity that clearly sets it apart from the previous ones. One of the set goals disappears during the negotiation process, in which one of the parties gains as their property the goals or actions mentioned by their adversary, which doesn't continue to defend their position.
- **The compromise:** It's when both parties reach a settlement without having their individual goals affected, meaning, an exchange of reciprocal contentment is made between the negotiators.

Improving oneself before the negotiation and learning their processes are a guarantee that the solutions or commitments that are established are satisfactory and beneficial for all parties.

Negotiation is based on the certainty that different options from the customary pattern can exist: "one wins and another one loses". You shouldn't try to start a fight, but to seek success and shared benefits.

To reach an agreement, it depends on the negotiation model of negotiation. The characteristic thing is that one actor makes an offer and the other makes a counter offer, publicly expressing the actions that will be performed, in a way that a settlement is reached.

It's necessary to clarify that the purpose of a negotiation process is not to bargain or recur to threats. If you don't manage to achieve a settlement, you should first introduce the arguments that support the proposal and observe the development of the process so that, in this way, you make decisions about how they will be handled to solve the conflict.

A negotiation isn't limited to the reach of the process. Every actor can impose elements and choose to withdraw when he deems it pertinent, as long as you're willing to make concessions even when they are not executed.

Reasons to negotiate

There are certain indicators who lead you to make a negotiation:

a. There exists an interest and profit for both parties, one wants to give in and the other one wants to get the service. At this point, in which there is a clear goal for each party, they just have to agree on the conditions that both actors present to continue with the negotiation process.

b. Obtaining a better settlement, when you know

this can be perfected in the negotiation.

c. You receive a claim, request or demand from an actor, raising a point to solve a specific problem. It's important to pay special attention to the claims so that they can be immediately solved without them extending and making the unsatisfied party to increase the problem.

d. You've received a negative as an answer, and that's all you need to start the negotiation process and that way changing the other person's decision to another one which achieves accordance in both parties.

e. There's a clear disagreement between both parties, which seems like a lie, but it's the normal thing when two or several actors exist in the middle of a choice. Each one has its own perspective and interest in the presented situation, when they should recur to a negotiation, trying as much as possible to satisfy both parties' requirements and avoid to put someone's benefit above the other's.

The negotiation process, mostly, is a complex path which presents many concerns, different arguments and point of views; and that's why it's necessary to use this resource.

Most negotiations often disintegrate before reaching the closure stage, which can bring consequences and unfavorable results for one of the parties, like time, lost money, and the possibility of not gaining a great benefit.

The breaking off in a negotiation can happen for several reasons:

- If the counterpart hasn't fulfilled the established duties.
- By discerning remarkable information that was not exposed at the time by the person who was obliged to do so.
- The illegality of the future business.
- The terms arising from a supervening event that impairs the continuation of a process or calls into question the benefit of the operation.

- The inability of one of the negotiators.
- The other competitive proposals who offer a greater benefit.
- A greater force or an unforeseen event.
- A modification in the economic or market conditions which affect the operation in a negative way.
- For unanimous decision for both parties or if there is any irremediable disagreement.
- The terms in which, evidently, insufficient possibilities of success can be predicted, tending to the few progresses in the negotiation or the disagreements between the parties.

Many times, a negotiation can break off just because of your ego and not due to the previously mentioned possibilities. Even if you think you're gaining an advantage, the company you represent might be losing. Most of the time, it's more affordable to reach an agreement than not reaching it and continue to dilate the process. A fact that must be clear is that every party values their position in a different way.

For instance, let's see the conversation between two office partners:

* *Excuse me, but you've parked your car twice in my spot. I say it to you nicely, without getting angry.*
* *I've only parked it there once.*
* *I'm sorry, but it's been twice.*
* *It's not such a big deal, man. Don't be like that.*
* *Don't be like that? Listen, I wouldn't be like this if you hadn't parked so many times in my spot.*
* *Hey, I don't like your tone.*
* *You don't like my tone? Which tone are you talking about? Well, I don't like your lack of companionship.*
* *It's you who lacks companionship, I've grown tired of you. You think you own that spot.*

Reasons to plan the negotiation

Before you start a negotiation, you must collect certain information and elaborate strategies that we'll explain in detail further on. Many people think that this process is simply selling or offering services and products, for which you must clarify that negotiating isn't selling.

Negotiation is about reaching exchanges and agreements which, possibly, benefit both parties. So that this cause is successful, you must properly plan it, so that the process is accomplished:

- **Decrease in errors:** It will be reduced to minimal possibilities of accepting terms which aren't beneficial or don't represent the closure of a bad agreement, without accepting non-negotiable elements or giving into pressure.
- **Stress reduction:** "Knowledge is power". By having previous information to the negotiation, you'll face it with greater confidence, reacting in an efficient way.
- **Win resistance:** Since you already have a clear view of negotiation, you'll have the strength to face the arguments and situations that come up.
- **Avoid possible professional failures** in situations in which you may present a lack of information and experience, communication skills or ignorance about a negotiation process.
- **Keep control of the situation,** you know what's the direction you must take, what you can offer and what you can't take. Meaning, correctly lead the negotiation.
- **You save time.** Even if you've invested a lot in planning the process of negotiation, preparing correctly will save you a lot of time because you handle certain information and you know what is and what isn't without the need of getting stuck in some goal without a founda-

tion.
- **You achieve better results** giving in valuable aspects for the counterpart, but less expensive for them and their customer.

CHAPTER 6
LEADERSHIP AND CHARISMA

There are three things that the speaker must contribute: showing, moving, delighting.

(Quintilian, *Institutes of oratory*, III, 5, 2)

Leadership isn't as simple and, like a negotiation, it depends on the surroundings in which it's developed, having as its primary function to motivate, organize, intervene and many times influence on choices and actions, which are carried out to achieve clear and precise goals.

It represents an opportunity to develop the potential of an individual, facing the different situations and challenges which will assess the ability they have to influence and motivate.

A leader who is able to influence directly on other people. It's not just about being the boss, it's about knowing how to lead a group in the management of situations or development of common goals, knowing how to exploit and power the different skills and abilities inherent to each of the people who make up the work team.

One of the outstanding characteristics from someone with good leadership is that they reach whatever goals they set for themselves. Generally, it's an intelligent person that shows security and firmness in their choices, they have the discipline to do almost anything and they easily adapt to their work environment. Characteristics which, joined by empathy and persuasion, are essential so that a person carries out a negotiation.

A leader must have the following skills:

- **Thoroughness,** taking care of every detail and stopping to analyze as many times necessary.
- **Honesty,** the strongest quality of every good leader; having clearly defined principles and values will help them lead the project correctly.
- **Motivating good communication among the work team** is a fundamental key to achieve success.
- **Keeping a positive mind** will help you draw knowledge out of any kind of situation during the process, watching for the silver lining.
- **Delegating,** being aware that you have a work team, and not wanting to do everything for yourself. A good leader knows who he can assign specific tasks to, trusting their abilities
- **Establish strategies,** in a way that the productivity levels increase and you can keep a balance between the workload and its results, without affecting your social and personal life.
- **Inspire,** motivate and deliver passion, focus on keeping a good mood in the work team.
- **Weight out the accomplishments and give credit when it's necessary,** since all the people who perform their job efficiently are hoping to be recognized and that their achievements are shown, which will boost their confidence and motivate the rest of the team to keep going and reach that acknowledgement at some point.
- **Align** the executable deadlines of the goal, focusing the team to set short and long-term objectives.
- **Guiding,** it's important to know the difference between being a leader and being a boss. A leader works well in teams, guides and directs through teachings and advices; while a boss only seeks to get results, sometimes imposing their will over the goals' achievement, without caring about the process or how the result was obtained.
- **Motivate good habits,** encouraging your team to have a balanced and healthy lifestyle, with positive and productive attitudes.

- **Encourage growth** through personal and professional development of their team.
- **Keep a neutral position**, without favorites, showing respect and cordial treatment towards everyone, equally.

One of the things that we must clarify, before carrying on with development, is that being a good leader isn't about assigning tasks to your team so that they do the work and you limit yourself to assess the results. The leader, aside from assigning, guiding and supervising, must be there during the whole process and be a part of it in order to develop it.

Hans Finzel stated that "a leader takes people to places they would've never gone to by themselves".

Even though leadership seems like an easy task, it's not that simple. A good leader will always be followed depending on the type of leadership they exert, and among them we find:

- **Authoritarian or transactional leadership:** This is a leader who's focused on conquering clearly established goals, ordering and expecting their mandates are fulfilled. An authoritarian leader assumes the decision-making and leans on punishments or rewards, trying to get their team's obedience.

They think they're the only person able to direct and control, they tend to impose their decisions and they mistrust their subordinates' abilities; they're not usually communicative and they struggle with delegating tasks.

One might argue that this type of leadership presents some advantages, like efficiency, short-term results, and the fulfillment of what is required. They're people who can work under pressure and make fast and correct decisions.

"Power isn't control. Power is strength and is giving that strength to others. A leader isn't someone who forces others in order to become stronger" (Beth Revis).

- **Formative or instrumental leadership:** It's a leader who motivates, who takes into account the interests, necessities and abilities of all members of the team, helping them develop their abilities and skills, orienting them to constant learning.

A good formative leader has an ease of expression and communication, they pay careful attention to arguments and the exposition of ideas of their team, they support and integrate everyone's thoughts, they insist on constant professional formation, they have didactic and methodological domain, they're assertive and empathetic.

"A good leader takes people where they want to go. A great leader takes them not necessarily where they want to go, but where they should be" (Rosalynn Carter).

- **Apathic leadership:** It's a leader who is elusive and scowling, they can delegate tasks but they're not interested in motivating or forming their team. They limit themselves to give instructions of the job and deadlines, without telling what is the path to achieve the goal.

This type of leadership presents problems in the group's coordination, doesn't achieve the team's integration nor does it provide any type of motivation, it struggles with foreseeing problems.

"A good leader is not stuck behind their desk" (Richard Branson).

"The art of communication is the leadership's language" (James Humes).

- **Motivating leadership:** Its main quality is charisma, they give off a lot of security, confidence and control; they're responsible and clear in their goals, they worry about the evolution of the whole team and acknowledge the achievements accomplished in conjunction.

It's an organized, communicative and committed person, trying to make their team have the same development and learning as them.

"A true leader is confident enough to be alone, courageous enough to make tough decisions and compassionate enough to listen to other people's needs. They don't set themselves to be a leader, but they turn into one due to their actions and the integrity of their intentions" (Douglas MacArthur).

A proper leadership offers you a lasting success, whole confidence in achieving the goals you set and observing, at the same time, the abilities and the progress of the maximum potential of their team, visualizing the transcendental changes generated.

Leadership is a neutral action, your way of leading will get the impact you decide and will progress or reduce based on the decisions you make.

Charisma is a trait of the personality based on feelings and values that, in some people can be an innate characteristic and in others a developed skill, with which the person has the ability to motivate, inspire and fascinate with their grace and charm.

There are many managers who have great knowledges, but don't possess the charisma to connect with the group they lead, they don't earn their trust easily and it's hard for them to have empathy, identifying as a transactional leader, not having the same efficiency when achieving goals as a charismatic leader would.

A charismatic leader is one who manages to cause enthusiasm in their group, who stands out for their energetic way of working, oftentimes, they're inspiring, visionary people who make good use of non-verbal communication. Their main traits are:

- Create admiration in their employees.
- Has a great persuasion ability.
- Take risks easily.
- They have conviction ability.
- They often use non-conventional but innovative mediums.
- They have a positive personality which generates trust.

The challenge of a charismatic leader is to achieve

that their team tends to their orders without feeling manipulated by their charm.

People say that a leader must have charisma and develop the charismatic leadership tactics (CLT), with which they achieve more influence and confidence to assume this role in a team. According to some studies, these tactics, compared to others which are commonly used for the structuring of the speech, the use of a comprehensible language and pronunciation clarity, they stick out as tools for checking who is a leader and not just a competent and trustable person.

The charismatic leadership tactics (CLT), though they are very effective, they're not known. Some leaders have practiced it without having knowledge of them, in ordinary situations which take place during the day.

The CLT aren't only useful when managing work teams on a company level, these tactics can be applied in any type of communication or teaching with the purpose of establishing emotional bonds with other people to be able to turn yourself into a competent, respected and powerful guide.

The charismatic leadership tactics are:

Connect, compare, contrast: One of the functions of a charismatic leader is getting their spectators to assimilate, understand and remember the supplied information.

The tools used to accomplish this are the use of metaphors, analogies and similes, of stories and anecdotes which manage to emotionally bond with the team, identifying with the leader; and contrasts which allow to clarify positions, comparing them to opposite actions through passion and reason, and, in some cases, dramatic touches.

"When management told me about it, it was like when I received the news of a pregnancy I had wanted for a very long time. The small difference is that, instead of waiting nine months, we only had four to be ready". This metaphor was exposed to a work team so that they perceived that in four months they'd be facing an uncomfortable situation that would end up being satisfying.

Implies and condenses: A charismatic leader uses rhetoric questions a lot, not expecting answers in return, they just ask them to reaffirm their point of view or reinforce the one of the interrogate; it's a tactic which is commonly used in friendly conversations, with our couples, in any time or situation.

This type of tool is often used when you seek to give a critic comment with an ironic tone, if it's about a reprimand. It can also be used when closing a speech or simply as an argument.

"Do you believe this is what I expected from your performance? Is this all you have to offer or do you feel like you're capable enough to move forward?"

Another commonly used tool in this tactic is the one of the tripartite lists, which act as a good persuasion method, offering three points which are easy to remember and enough to defend the business itself.

Show integrity, authority and passion: It's about portraying confidence that the objectives can be accomplished, transmitting the passion and vision to reach them. The expressions of moral security and affirmations show a sentiment of the group, implanting the authority and credibility of the leader, and at the same time, achieving the alignment and identification of the team with their guide.

The arguments and positive, motivational messages which are expressed with energy and passion, are the ones who reach the work team the most, helping to infect them with the spirit of overcoming.

Charisma in voice and body: Another tool that should be worked very well is the use of the three non-verbal signals. It's looking out for what's being transmitted through our face, our body and our voice. Not all leaders have a good control of this aspect, but it's something they can learn and put into practice.

Facial expressions: They must be visible to those

who observe you. Through them, you reinforce the message you wish to convey. Try to maintain eye contact and learn how to feel well with your cackles and smiles, when you frown or any other spontaneous gesture.

Variations in the voice: A good speaker plays with the sounds or tones of their voice, they know when to raise their voice and when to whisper, they perfectly manage emotions through the sound of their words and control the pauses, using them only at the right moments.

Gestures: They help showing the message, illustrating it, managing to accentuate it and transmitting it easily.

Incorporating these charismatic leadership tactics will bring you a clear benefit when using them in your presentation and speeches, it's just a matter of preparing, rehearsing them and practicing them. You can start by using some during individual conversations, which make you feel more comfortable and which are spontaneous.

Some exercises that can be helpful are to record yourself and then analyze and self-criticize what you must improve, or do it at home with your partner and friends. With time and expertise, you'll start using them fluidly.

It's not necessary to apply each and every one of the tactics at all meetings, conversations or activities which require it, you just have to use those which you think are convenient at specific times in a combined and balanced way. Don't think that, not being charismatic by nature, you won't be able to learn charismatic leadership tactics, you just have to work hard to understand them, use them and practice them.

CHAPTER 7
THE MAIN STYLES OF NEGOTIATION

Without philosophy the eloquent speaker that we seek can't be formed, not in the supposition however, that in it you'll find everything, but that it can help as the stage does the actor; since oftentimes, very rightly, the small is compared to the big. Effectively, without philosophy nobody could talk about important and varied subjects with enough extension and profanity.

(Cicero, *De Oratore*, 4, 14-15)

In a negotiation all the people who intervene face different attitudes and personal ways of carrying out the process; this is what the strategies and styles of negotiation represent.

When reasoning and knowing the motives of the different styles of negotiation that exist, you can prepare strategies according to the attitudes of the counterpart with the goal of achieving success in the negotiation.

The style of negotiation not only depends on the personal attitudes of the involved people, you must also consider who you are negotiating with, if it's a subordinate or a superior, an amateur, a naive or an expert. There are many factors which intervene when it comes to negotiating. There isn't a type of direct personality related to the success that can be obtained in the exchange, but you must be aware of the experience and nature of the person as well as the analysis previous to the process.

Some personality elements that affect the behavior and the results in a negotiation are:

- **Authoritarianism:** when you try to impose ideas and goals.
- **Anxiety:** We feel nervousness, concern or worry at the beginning and during the negotiation.
- **Cognitive complexity:** When it's difficult to understand the intuitive way to proceed in negotiation.
- **Level of self-esteem;** It shows the level of security or insecurity that is presented during the process of negotiation.
- **Dogmatism:** They struggle with accepting that their ideas, opinions or affirmations are judged; the way they see it, they're not wrong in their position.
- **Propensity to risks**: They see chances in taking risks in the face of conflict, commitments, among others, to get better profit at the end. They're usually optimistic people.
- **Tendency to conciliation:** They try to make a pact or settlement in a peaceful and harmonious way.
- **Suspicion:** they suspect any attitude and they frequently see others' bad intentions, they don't trust the counterpart.

Other characteristics which influence your personal style for negotiation, and aren't least important, are the cultural social baggage each one has. The way you relate and socialize says a lot about the human quality you possess.

The main styles of negotiation used are:

Evasive Style

They try to retreat or revoke the process, which can be very prejudicial especially if we talk about businesses with little experience. The negotiator with this style tries as hard as possible to avoid conflicting situations trying to eliminate prejudice during the process.

To use this style, the negotiator must give the impression of not knowing the model of business of the company and not having a defined approach; they can get to ignore a conflict in a partial or total way.

The personality of the invasive negotiator leads them not assume a hook situation, the control center is external and they tend to present a lower level of assertiveness; they make sarcastic comments, throw tantrums in moments of anger, and they keep from speaking about the subject without having to make relevant decisions

This style can be harmful since it can trigger the loss of benefits and business opportunities. If there is no responsibility, there isn't a response value

"Never negotiate from fear and never fear negotiating" (John F. Kennedy).

Contentious competitive Style

It presents strong and determined positions for which the main goal is success regardless of the future relationship between the parties, which means that when using this style of negotiation, you intend to win at all costs and under any circumstances.

It's an aggressive style with which the negotiator involves themselves in any conflict opportunity, being their main focus to win and to watch the other party lose. The negotiator is a person who is constantly defensive, they criticize, no matter if they're constructive or destructive, they try to obstruct the process if they see that it's detouring from the way they wished to take, which depending on their ethics and morals can present violent situations and use traps.

Their behavior can be machiavellian, hostile and mistrusting, they don't change their convictions in the face of pressure, they can be selfish, manipulative and use repressive tactics without showing any consideration for the other party

It's commonly used by companies who control a wide market and who can influence in the apparition of new competitors whether they're direct or indirect ones. The economic factor is the most saved and protected point and it's the only thing they care about.

It's a recommended technique for circumstances in which you only perform a negotiation and it's not in your interest to take care of future relationship between the parties.

"Do what you can to know who you're facing. Never sit down to deal with a stranger." (Somers White).

Adapting-yield style

The behavior of this style is giving and yielding; even if they're not completely satisfied with the result of a negotiation, they offer a part of what they want, on the counterpart's request, without completely giving up their needs.

With this negotiation style you're avoiding to do other possible negotiations, it's a neutral position in the face of the conflict that is being presented.

The personal characteristics of this type of negotiator are the necessity to have an external control center, the need for company and pleasing other people.

The negotiator adopts a patient, conciliatory and even submissive behavior when facing their counterpart, many times being aware that they won't achieve the best results. Having this attitude can represent instability between the needs of one party and the other one. Despite of the risks that this style creates, it's sometimes used by some entrepreneurs to get into new markets and achieve the permanence of the relationships in the future.

Among the techniques used in this style of negotiation we can find the decrease of the projected prices, the acceptance of payment conditions, being favorable or not to the company; in some cases, it can even come to delivering information of interest. It's not convenient to keep this style in a persistent way.

"The biggest of dangers for most of us is not that our

goal is too high and that we don't reach it, but that it's way too low and we accomplish it" (Miguel Angel Bounarroti).

Cooperative collaborative Style

Unlike the previous style, in this one you find the way in which both parties get what they want, in which every one of them has the best position and attitude so they can reach a beneficial settlement and end in good terms. It also receives the name of integrator or cooperative negotiation.

In this model of negotiation, you take into account the needs of both parties in the same way, it's ideal for those companies who want to establish noticeable relationships in the market, which start their operations and intend to keep good relationships through the course of time. In some cases, in negotiations with this style you obtain more profit than planned.

The negotiator who uses this style often has a high emotional stability and a great need for accomplishments, added to competitiveness.

This style of negotiation happens successfully when there are common goals and objectives, showing an assertive and flexible attitude, trying as much as possible to avoid conflicts which obstruct a favorable ending for both parties.

"My father used to say that you didn't have to keep all the money there was in a deal, because then, if you earn a reputation for keeping all the money, there wouldn't be any more deals" (Jean Paul Getty).

Flexible Style

It's a style used to reach a concrete solution in a fast way. Concrete objectives are dealt with without touching the marrow bone of the case or structural items. It's about reaching solutions and settlements which are fair and balanced for all the people involved.

The personality of this negotiator is presented as a conciliator, objective and focused person.

It's extremely useful when you're new in the market and you want to avoid losing sales or customers.

This type of negotiation is recommended for short periods of time, meaning, temporarily.

"Negotiating is discovering what the other party really wants and show them the way to get it, while you get what you want" (Alejandro Hernández).

To achieve a successful negotiation, it's essential that the involved people have knowledge of the importance the final result of the negotiation has, as well as the type of process and durability of the relationship between the parties.

In negotiations, each party can use the style they think is convenient and which allows them to achieve their goal, making an efficient and absolute analysis of the different scenarios that might happen, the conditions of the process and the diverse criteria which will be generated, keeping in mind that there would be moments in which it's necessary to improvise, reform or decipher the opposite strategy.

Now that we've seen the different styles that can be adopted in a negotiation, it's important to distinguish some elements which directed influence each and every one of them:

- **Expectations:** by keeping the possibility or hope of achieving the wanted result, and respecting the level of the counterpart, the negotiation can be more cooperative and fluid. Otherwise, if a high expectation is kept with little margin of movement during the negotiation process, it will turn competitive, generating tension between the actors.
- **Unique or continuous negotiation character:** if you want a lasting relationship after the negotiation and to achieve great benefits for both parties, you must

accomplish a model of cooperation; but if the negotiation happens for that one time, the most likely thing is that the style turns practical and executable, meaning, concrete, regardless of the type of relationships generated (it is not important).

- **Negotiation climate:** it's related to the level of confidence, the attitudes and the security in which both parties negotiate.
- Time pressure, power, social structure.
- Denial context.

The possible situations which come up in a negotiation and depending on the style being used can be:

➢ Of confrontation: the counterpart's interests are not considered; the goal is to fix the conflict by leaning on the terms imposed by the other party.

➢ Of cooperation: it's about finding beneficial solutions for everyone involved in the negotiation, focusing on identifying the center of the problem.

➢ Of subordination: you make partial or total concessions, allowing some aspects.

➢ Of inaction: it represents delaying any action that led to the solution of the conflict.

➢ Of retreat: no action or posture is taken in a definite way and any conflictive situations or polemics are avoided.

"Listening to others offers you the possibility to have a more objective and complete vision about the subject which interests you, aside from providing you with the opportunity of creating an environment of mutual collaboration instead of one of conflict" (Tony Buzan).

Oftentimes, several styles can be used in the same negotiation, since complicated situations happen which wrap up several businesses. There isn't one style of negotiation that is more convenient than the other.

CHAPTER 8
INTERESTS AND GOALS IN THE NEGOTIATION

The same necessity of speaking makes us express and draw out even the most difficult thought, and the burning desire of living increases the favorable impulses.

(Quintilian, *Institutes of oratory*, X, 7, 17)

The settlement in a negotiation is the means to give a response and solution to our interests, it's clearly a part of the negotiation's goals, but it's not the final objective.

There are four types of objectives which make up a negotiation:

- The objectives of desires of profit. **(G)**.
- The objectives of relationship between interests and goals which can be found in important points **(R)**.
- The objectives related to ego, necessities, dignity and self-esteem goals. **(I)**.
- The objectives of process, the style to be used **(P)**.

The GRIP can change during and after a negotiation. During this process, interruptions can happen to analyze new information, assessing the initial information once again or verify a change in the objectives. Meaning, sometimes, it's ideal to make a new analysis in order to clear the path and the possible result of the negotiation. Retrospection can be very useful for a proper work during the whole process

It's important that these goals are classified and identified taking into account every one of the involved people's point of views during the negotiation, because this will allow you to obtain the necessary information to choose and develop the right strategies, and it will help us meet the common points looking for mutual benefits.

Aspirations for profit (G): they represent tangible, common interests in a conflict which are fundamental, like the objective. Recognizing them in the opposite party is desirable, since they're easy to find out. The external goals depend on the vision you have, meaning if you have a negative vision, it's normal to think that the counterpart's objectives disagree with ours, which is fake. It's true that every individual has their own desires and interests, but in a negotiation, it often happens that we make suppositions about the alternative, viable goals of both parties, leading them to common points which benefit the most valuable goals for everyone.

"Examples of G objectives can be to graduate in the corresponding time from your career, finding a job according to your ability and specialization, a salary which fits the work position, managing to deliver a project within the deadline"

Relationship objectives (R): these are focused on the type of relationship that you wish or want to maintain, representing the value and nature of that relationship, with the people involved in the process of negotiation. These objectives can turn out to be a little more difficult to identify than the profit objectives.

In few words, this objective refers to the quality and type of handle that the person has with one or both parties.

"Example of the R objectives; Luis is appointed a project leader and he has a multidisciplinary team to his disposal, his superior assigns him the project and gives him a deadline for the following month. Two people in the team are newly graduates, they don't use the programs for the accomplishment of the project Luis decides to divide the group in two parts; the first is made up by him and the two newly graduates, the second is composed by the two most experienced people. He divides the tasks according to the abilities and he delivers the project on established deadline".

G objective: Luis keeps his position and he delivers the project in the established time.

R objective: Luis fulfilled and has an excellent relationship with his boss and the team. In the process, he offered teachings to the two newly graduates, who are completely grateful and committed to Luis, since he didn't displace them, and integrated them and appreciated their efforts.

SELF objectives (I): They are congruent with the relationship objectives. They're about our self-esteem, the necessity to increase our ego, the fears we have; anyways, the perception you have of yourself.

These objectives can be competitive and rigid when putting the self before someone else's self-esteem, which is why it's important to know how to recognize them to be able to control your ego and use the other person's SELF in a positive and constructive way, accepting that everyone is worthy of respect and acknowledgement.

"An example of the SELF objectives; if we set ourselves on the previous example, depending on Luis' ego, behavior and self-esteem, it's possible to draw SELF objectives which can be seen as positive or negative.

Positive SELF objectives Luis wants to be seen as someone who fixes problems; intelligent, efficient, effective, a fair person who respects and values, expecting to be treated in the same way.

Negative SELF objectives: he doesn't want to be seen as an incompetent, he's afraid of looking like a fool or a failure and he doesn't want to lose. Having as a G objective a promotion or a production bonus."

Process objectives (P): they can be affected by the previous objectives and their surroundings, they specify the way in which you expect a negotiation to proceed, they can have either a constructive approach as a destructive one, and integral or distributive.

In these objectives the participation of the parties is

included, the procedures and the style of communication they have. The more parties are involved, the bigger will be the difficulty to reach a settlement and the options to develop it.

The personality and attitude that all the involved parties have, directly affects the P objectives, analyzing which process can be practical, safe and positive, and help reach a settlement. Sometimes, the first deal that must be looked for inside a negotiation is how the procedure itself will be.

"The process is essential even in two-party negotiations, no matter how simple the affair is. If one of the parties leaves the negotiation table feeling like they weren't allowed to stand their position or were forced to reach a settlement, they might not proceed. This party can undo the agreement, which will be followed by a new conflict".[2]

A negotiation process is determinant to all the parties' interaction, it might be more important than the settlement itself. If one of the parties perceives the process as improper, clearly, the settlement won't be taken in a good way and it'll take away the possibility to be correctly accepted.

In a process you can emphasize the differences of the predecessor power or dissipate authority, it can be a directive a competitive process.

"Example of P process; Luis chose a constructive approach and a distributive style; he chose to be the directive authority making a competition of abilities within the team."

---

[2] Budjac, B. *Techniques of negotiation and conflict resolution*, page. 114.

Classification and assessment of the objectives

It's a very important, necessary and effective step in every negotiation. Studies made about which objectives are relevant and compatible and which aren't, aside from finding common points, fast solutions and starting systematic plan.
- Identifying and classifying the interests and goals.
- They must be analyzed in a thorough way.
- Assume a systemic approach, analyzing all the contextual factors and the interrelation.
- Observing all the additional objectives and the connected consequences of what has to be achieved.

Change of objectives

During or after the negotiation process the objectives can be changed, including the perceptions of the people involved and determination of dissatisfaction with the process. By changing them, new objectives come up, which correspond to the information that has been updated, accepting that the objectives previously set are unattainable.

- **Prospective objectives:** They make up the specific intentions that want to be fulfilled and that can be communicated. They represent those that are established at the beginning of the negotiation.

"Luis needs to finish the project, he communicates his team that they have an exact month before the deadline, which was conjunctly decided with his superior"

- **Retrospective objective:** they can help us with future interactions and turn out to be complicated and confusing, but it's necessary to understand their behaviors and decisions based on them. One particular variety of these objectives is that they can lead us to self-sabotage and make us believe that what didn't turn out lacks importance and value, and what did turn out is better than the expected. Dignity and rationalization are used.

- One of the scenarios that Luis plans is that the project isn't fulfilled in a month. It turns out that, in fact, it wasn't fulfilled and it was extended for another month, the schedule wasn't met and Luis was removed from his position.

Luis thinks that it was for the best, in his new position he has less responsibility and he has the same salary that he had when he had to take care of a whole team.

The objectives and strategies of negotiation lead us to classify and identify in a clear and precise way our own objectives and the counterpart's, managing to make the GRIP template to develop the planning of the entire negotiation process.

The GRIP objectives give you the possibility to choose if it's necessary to go to the negotiation, taking the decision of avoiding or solving the conflict. The GRIP facilitates the choice of how to get where you want to be, knowing exactly what you want. It's a very useful tool for achieving successful results.

"If you want to improve your dialectic position in a dialog or negotiation, you must stimulate the active participation of your interlocutors. And not only because you will convey your education and rigor, but because your rivals will tend to make verbal excesses" (José Luis Rodríguez Jiménez).

CHAPTER 9
THE PROPOSAL

Three things the speaker needs to look at: what to say, in what occasion and in which way.

(Cicero, *De Oratore*, 14, 42-43)

When we want to persuade or negotiate with someone who has opposite ideas to ours, it's necessary to present a proposal. What does this proposal consist of?

A proposal is basically an idea or a project which is presented to someone else so that they accept it. It's an offer on our part so that this person accepts something different to what they have in mind.

To propose something, you must make sure you know two things: the first is knowing what the other person wants and the second is knowing their priorities. Making a proposal isn't something that must be taken lightly, as every action, since it's very likely that it'll have consequences, what you must try to achieve, if possible, is that they're positive for both parties. If you don't know what the other party wants, there would be no way that you can make a proposal that adapts and is close to what you're both looking for.

Generally, when negotiating in a first instance, we don't state specifically what our intentions are, in order to leave the wide field accessible to for the other person in which they can express their ideas, and this of course will give us a clear picture of their intentions. Besides, it's a way of not letting them know our objectives so when we open the possibility that they make us a proposal which will be equally or more lucrative than what we were expecting.

For instance, many times it happens that when a person is asked what the cost of their services are, the answer will be "I'd like to know what's your base budget". Do you know why they do this? So, they know how much the other person is willing to pay, because they think "what if I say $100 and they're willing to pay $150?"; what they're looking for is a way of earning as much as possible.

The thing is, though it might seem like a good idea, it actually isn't. What happens is that we take a risk, because the possibilities are not as favorable as we think, we have a 45% probability that they offer something that we're not interested in, a 45% possibility that the offer is something lesser than what we're interested in, and only a 10% probability that the proposal is better to what we were expecting. So, we really should be clear about what it is we need and how we're going to get it.

What things do I have to keep in mind when making a proposal to negotiate?

Always bring a proposal to the negotiation table

Generally, we struggle with establishing a proposal. What we always expect is that the other person starts to see what they're aiming for. I repeat to you, this is a mistake, every time you negotiate you must do so with a clear picture of what you want, and this implies to structure your proposal and working hard on it to achieve it.

It's very rare that when starting a negotiation, you get what you want or even more, but what it is most likely is that during the exchange of ideas, you achieve it, that's why you must have something structured to present to the other party. It's the only way to win, is to seem confident and clear about what you want.

Be clear about what you want

When we start negotiating with empty hands, we give

the other person the power to handle us within their proposal. The only way that this works is that we don't know what we want and that we look for support in the information that the other party might provide us with. But what happens if those expectations aren't anywhere near to what you look for? You probably have to convince the other person to raise their offer, and it's at that point that everything becomes, more than a negotiation, a struggle for power.

Another important matter is that when the other party is the one making the approaches, you must be skillful and quick to think about the "why" of their proposal, what is its purpose. When receiving a proposal always apply thinking about it coldly, don't start negotiating immediately. Remember that a proposal from the other party is always supported on their needs, not necessarily on yours; which is why it's important that you're always clear about what you want and how you want to sell it to the other person.

Gather the information and move forward

When you need to propose something, the first thing you must do is study the surroundings, see what other offers, and similar areas to yours there are; this is the way to know the market and stomp firmly when you negotiate.

Negotiations always move forward supported on proposals, not in arguments. When you're based on arguments, you're practically defending yourself and not trying to come up with a solution for the other party. Remember that it's not only about what you want, but reaching a settlement with the other person, performing a process of exchange. Subjectivity, in these cases has no room because, more than helping, what it does is complicate the process.

"You move forward with questions and proposals, never with opinions and arguments. Defending your own argument will stop you from making proposals. The more you argue, the more will the other person argue. The more you push the other person, the more you'll be pushed. Invest your time in coming up with solutions and exchange information. Run away from ironic and sarcastic behaviors. Don't try to score in front of everyone.".[3]

Take the initiative and set the pace

Your proposal must always be completely realistic. If you're clear about what you want and you have strong arguments to prove that it's not madness, the best thing you can do is take the initiative and start the negotiation for yourself, this will give you an advantage to set the rules of the game and, of course, it will be very positive to direct the way of a negotiation and picking the right moment.

Always, the person who directs the conversation is the one who begins with stating their proposal. A good way of setting a foundation is through the formulation of questions, doing so directly will give you the answers you need in a quick way. You must always ask one question at a time, doing several at the same time will give the other person the possibility to answer what's convenient for them; on the other hand, following this recommendation you'll get information in a precise way. Another important thing is that you mustn't attack the other person with questions who sound heavy, for instance: Do you think I'm going to accept that? What do I get in return? Do you think I'm stupid? These types of questions are often annoying, so you better not ask them. Your speech must have a very respectful tone which promotes the fluidity of the negotiation, and not get in the way.

To approach the other person and get your proposal to be accepted, you must try not to be incisive with your

---

[3] Hernández, A. *Negotiating is easy, if you know how*, page 84.

answers: saying "yes" or "no" sharply, more than a way to clarify what you're doing, it's a way to slow down the other person. If it's absolutely necessary to reply with a "no", accompany it with a "yes" all the time. In a first instance, the word "no" will stop the expectations of the other person, but when it comes with a "yes" you'll give them a choice and this will be positive for the negotiation. If you give "no" as an answer and you don't say anything else, you'll be giving power to the other person to propose and continue, in a way you'll be giving up the lead of the negotiation, and the idea is that you're the person who dominates it.

Another thing that you can do is stating, as an answer, something that you know they can fulfill or that it will be really difficult to perform. This strategy is very used by products salesmen. Since there are many careless people who don't keep a receipt or keep the box where the product came in good conditions, they use it to their advantage. It's a way of not telling them directly that they don't accept devolutions, so they find alternatives so that it's the customer who breaches, and at the end they can't ask for the return.

Specify the reach, but not how much you want it

Every time you make a proposal, focus on giving details of what it is that you want, and never reveal how important or significant it is for you, because you might give the other party tools to manipulate you based on this. Remember, doing the opposite is a mistake.

Additionally, it's clear that you must establish your priorities and know exactly what it is that you want and how you want it, but you shouldn't let the other person know because this can mean you can run the risk that they ignore part of your request for being considered less important.

Don't try to expose the other party, be realistic!

When you structure proposals, do it based on the reality of things, with solid and clear arguments. What happens when you don't? When you bring an unmeasured and unbelievable proposal, what you motivate is mistrust and, more than a dialogue, what you cause is a hostile environment in which the other person will only want to defend themselves. State realistic and coherent proposals in a clear and complete way. Don't start a situation that will play against you and that, surely won't lead you to the best terms.

Never accept a proposal in the first offer

This is a very common mistake. When something is proposed that meets our expectations, we say yes immediately and then we gloat on the negotiation skills that we have.

The situation has two faces: the first is that the other party often thinks that suddenly they could have offered less and you still would have accepted; and the other is yours, who after thinking things in a calmer way, you'll be having doubts about whether you could have gotten more out of that agreement. The most recommended thing is always to ask for an extra.

Keeping all of this in mind, then you must proceed to structure your proposal, it must be formed by two elements: terms and offers

The fact of making a proposal implies that you're going to perform a negotiation, and when you look to negotiate, you must give something in return. So, it's important, besides clearly establishing your reach and what it is that you want, bring an offer to make your arguments grow attractive in the eyes of the other party. You must do it in the most assertive way possible, and be firm and even in what you're exposing so that the other person sees confidence in you and they know that you're prepared and have a solid foundation that they won't be able to knock down easily even if they wanted to.

Show yourself strong and centered when making your proposal and always try to make your conditions complete, firm, but that your offer is ambiguous, this way you'll have flexibility in the offer that you'll present the other person.

When presenting a proposal, always unravel it by points, by everything you require, and then proceed to detail each and every one of them. But remember, the explanation must not be long, more like a specific one, so that the other party doesn't feel like you're trying to justify something that isn't really that good as you're trying to sell. Besides, it should always be accompanied with a proper body language, a good voice tone, and a correct posture so that you give it more solidity and acceptance.

To close up this chapter, I want to leave you a list with the different stages that might come up in a proposal and to which you must pay attention:

- *A negotiation moves forward with proposals.*
- *It doesn't move forward with arguments.*
- *The proposal defeats the argument.*
- *An argument prevents you from making a proposal.*
- *You can only negotiate concrete proposals.*
- *The opinions and arguments aren't negotiable.*
- *Interrupting leads you to an argument.*
- *With proposals you set your path.*
- *A proposal is composed of terms and offers.*
- *If you only have terms, you'll be imposing on the other person.*
- *If you only have offers, you'll be yielding.*
- *Open in a realistic way. Move forward with moderation.*
- *An unmeasured proposal will lead you to blockage.*
- *Step ahead of the other person with your proposal.*

- *Your proposal is reinforced if it invites to its response.*
- *Propose, explain and ask.*
- *Don't explain to people, it sounds like a justification.*
- *Be firm in the general stuff and flexible about the specific.*
- *Ask what they think of your proposal.*
- *Your terms must always be concrete.*
- *If your offer is always ambiguous, it'll earn flexibility.*
- *Your offer must always be conditional.*
- *Don't offer with the hope of a reciprocal move from the other party.*
- *Don't just complain, propose your solution.*
- *The worst answer to your proposal is a "yes".*
- *Don't grant anything on credit, collect it on the spot.*
- *From an argument you always walk out with proposals.*[4]

---

[4] Hernández, A. *Negotiating is easy, if you know how*, page. 102 y 103.

CHAPTER 10
RULES OF NEGOTIATION

The good sense, then, that every eloquent speaker, is adapting two times and people. Well, I esteem that not in front of everyone, nor against everybody, nor with everyone you talk in the same way. Those who accommodate their speech to the proper decorum of each thing will be eloquent. Once they've taken this for granted, they will say each thing as they should be said, not the abundant with poverty, nor the great thing with smallness, nor the other way around, but the style will go hand in hand and adequate to the subjects themselves.

(Cicero, *Da Oratore*, 35 y 36, 123)

In every negotiation two or more people's opinions are exposed to reach a positive agreement between the involved parties about a common affair to achieve a profit or benefit for both of them. Dialogue in a negotiation is necessary, but it can exist without the help of the other party. That's why, up next, a series of rules to make the debate more pleasant and interesting are described so that the established goals can be achieved.

The rules you must take into account when negotiating are:

You must prepare yourself to negotiate

If you want to guarantee success when negotiating, you must prepare yourself. It's the least thing that you need to face any challenge in life: preparation.

The fundamental thing is doing it about the goal that you need, not simply start exposing what you want without knowing which arguments or where you want to get.

You wouldn't be directing the request, but letting yourself be led by the counter attacker's offer. Having the approach clear, you'll be more alert to the opportunities and to face the obstacles that might come up in the dialogue, to the primary necessity of the possible arguments that the other person can use to raise doubts. In this way, if the adversary realizes that they black preparation when arguing an objective, they will become more confident and increase the expectations of what's most favorable for them.

Being more attentive to things that might come up and it's effectively and take advantage of opportunities is something that you must work on the deep down, you are not born with the talent for negotiation, preparation meets you to it which is why you should be prepared to negotiate and then only to defend a point of view.

Don't take it as a game

Many people believe that negotiation is the game with the rooms, without knowing that thinking this way they create a win-or-lose atmosphere stop. Negotiating isn't fun or a competition in which one person wins and the other person loses. This is not the right atmosphere to express ideas and reached an end. Perhaps if you think this way, many times you might believe that you've won, when in reality, you might be losing in advance if the counterpart can't fulfill their end of the bargain.

Learn to know the other party

It's fairly important to know the other person a little bit, what's their leadership, their behavior, any important aspect of their personality, just like their needs and how these can affect or not the end of said negotiation. In this way, you'll be attentive to what they might comment and you'll know how to respond or act in said case.

You must also take into account what the counterpart's opinion is, knowing which questions to ask in order to get their attention and find out what they think about a certain subject. This is a way of obtaining valuable information about the intentions or goals of the person that you wish to negotiate a certain affair with, getting the information from the main character themself.

Take into account that the more you make the other person talk so that they explain their point of view, the more information they'll be giving you about the firmness and position of the surroundings in which they move in and about their beliefs and thoughts.

Know your limits and necessities

You must be clear about what it is that you wish to obtain out of the negotiation and how far you can get to accomplish it. Realistically studying what you want, you'll know with which moderation to negotiate it.

We know our limitations and we always aspire to something lower than we can, it's us who block ourselves and don't let our mind set their ideal course. Knowing what we need and how far we're willing to go to get it, we avoid the negotiation to block and stop. As well as avoiding having to yield when you ask for too much and it's time to lower your guard, losing credibility in the dialogue. That's why the best thing to do is to act with moderation.

Have a list of common goals

So that the negotiation is more pleasant and it generates more trust and comfort, the best thing is to try and begin it by touching the points of interest for both parties, this way you'll manage to get their attention and make them see what they're trying to negotiate, not compete. The other party will notice that they'll be benefitted when touching on subjects that are interesting to them, and they will study or take into account what's requested to make an improvement on the subject that's being discussed.

When looking for objectives, at first, don't include those who might block the negotiation.

Para que no se olvide nada, realiza una lista con todos los puntos a tratar, comenzando por los comunes. Al momento de redactarla, se creativo y ten un orden de prioridades. Ante la presión de la negociación, puede que no se te ocurra nada, es por ello la importancia detener a la mano esta lista.

Learn to retreat when it's convenient

At times, a negotiation or a deal are death. Don't keep going with it out of strength of tenacity when you can't change the other person's perspective. This, more than being helpful, what it would do is wear you out and create a hostile situation with the other party. Sometimes it's necessary to know how to recognize when you must insist, but also, it's far more important to know when you must retreat. Even though we don't reach the best settlement, it's best to move forward a little bit with conversations.

If your assessment isn't correct or are incomplete to a point where you must review your objective, it's preferable to postpone it, since you're not prepared. Take the necessary time to analyze and prepare in the right way. If it's a low objective, then you'll learn something from this negotiation that you could use in the next negotiation.

Integrity and confidence in yourself are key

Inspiring confidence is crucial, since it maintains credibility. If the confidence the counterpart has in you weakens or is damaged during the negotiation, try to repair it immediately. Assume the responsibility of the consequences that have been caused because of you. Admit the perspective and apologize for the mistakes made.

It's at this point in which you have to use the persuasion methods if it ever happens that you can't convince the other person to yield for your ideas or if you've slightly damaged the trust and credibility that this person has in you. You must be skillful enough to repair the damage without the other party barely noticing it.

Learn to identify who to negotiate with

Imagine that you'll be negotiating an agreement to sign a time extension of a contract to paint an office. In a building where there are other companies working already, who must you negotiate with? The managers of the other companies? Of course not! You must do it with person who hired you, with whom you have enough authority to decide the timeline and the conditions of the extension, without running the risk that another one comes and break the agreement between the parties. You must not do it with the secretary or with the warehouse boss, no! you must do it with the project leader, the person responsible to establish the points and define priorities for the good functioning of the site.

If you try to reach a settlement with someone who has no authority to make a commitment, the negotiation will lead to an unpleasant situation, for you and even for both. It's important than by the end of the negotiation both parties are satisfied.

This is one of the most common points in which people fail when negotiating: doing so with the wrong person can delay the times without getting any profit for the parties. Besides, reaching a settlement with a non-authorized person is like having done nothing.

Perform a follow-up and leave everything on record

When you perform a negotiation is very important to elaborate a report of all the things that were accomplish and those with which no settlement was reached. Besides, write down what is the reach of the agreement, in a clear way, so that everything that has been discussed and the agreements made are on record.

You must also write down the subjects which are still open for debate. If the negotiation implies data or concrete specifications, it's very important that they're on record and both parties sign it. Don't leave out what it's not convenient for you to highlight or negotiate, this should be included because that way it will be incorporated to the document in a complete, exhaustive and correct way.

Remember that, as the saying goes, "words are gone with the wind". There's nothing more trustworthy and safer than making a document or a minute of all the treated in the meeting and, in the end, in a well specified way, every point of the endorsement of the signatures of each party are included as a symbol of their conformity and according to what has been stated in the document.

CHAPTER 11
STAGES AND TECHNIQUES OF

Men unable to speak often got the fruit of eloquence for the dignity of their action and many orators with ease of speech were deemed unable to speak because of their imperfection in action.

(Cicero, *Da Oratore*, 17, 55-56)

Before beginning to speak of the stages and techniques of negotiation, it's necessary that we understand the fundamental concepts which will help us understand everything about it.

We start with the style, the approach within the interaction. We have several styles of negotiators: those who use evasion, the person who arguments or competitive, the committed and the cooperative or collaborative.

There's also the counterpart, which is a commonly used term inside a negotiation because it's the component of one of the parties to perform the negotiation. It's also known as the opponent.

Another one of the concepts related to the negotiation are the tactics or maneuvers, which are defined as the actions which can be taken to win said negotiation. The tactics in a negotiation include questions, tolerance, postponement, surprise, retreat, threats, anger, revocation, exclusion or enclosure, cowering, deceive, distraction, reluctance, bargaining, ultimatum, association, equalization, request, harassment, laughter, extrapolation, exaggeration, extreme positions, patience, blocking, counteroffers, concessions, restrictions and silence.

We can also talk of the gambits, a representation used to refer to the maneuvers designed with the purpose of achieving some kind of leverage. This term comes from chess and is often used in the language of negotiation.

And finally, we have the technique which refers to how you use the tactics and alternative or multiple gambits in negotiation.

When we talk of the stages of negotiation it's very useful to examine this whole process in five stages. These are known as the preparation, introductory or exploration, initiation or proposal, intensification or exchange, and closure or settlement stages.

To have an effective negotiation each of its stages are very important, for this reason, we will study them in detail.

Preparation stage

Preparation is the most difficult part of the whole process of negotiation. After determining and analyzing the nature of the problem, it's necessary to start the preparations of the tactics that will be applied to solve the conflict. The first question you must ask yourself is what do you expect to achieve, this will allow you to prepare to react to the opponent's movements. Always keep in mind that, without preparation, you won't get good results.

You must always know in depth the subject being discussed, since if your opponent realizes that you don't know what you're talking about or that you have basic knowledge, as a consequence the confidence in themselves will increase and it will be harder to achieve a victory, and they'll even dare asking for more.

Introductory or exploration stage

This stage can be unraveled in the following steps:

1. Realize and explore what the other one wants.

2. Defining the rules and establishing the tone through the formulation of questions to listen and understand what the other person wants. Listen to your opponent's replies even if some things bother you.

3. Focus on the matters. Tell the other person what you want to get, don't tell them how bad you want to get it.

4. Start convincing your opponent with the right tactics, using a style and technique which adapts to their strategy and personality. You must be attentive to the opposite's signals; the most important thing is that you have to be clear about what the other person wants to know how to reply. Prepare a summary of what the counterpart wants and assess which options can help you during the negotiation.

One of the first steps for a good negotiation is establishing the tone for it. You start with a data identification, such as names, positions or professions, business of the company or firm, among others.

In this stage you must establish personal contact so that your opponents trust you. Try to convey an attitude and always maintain dignity and respect.

Initiation or proposal stage

The main aspect of this stage is asking. Questions are used during the whole negotiation process due to the fact that it's extremely important to get as much information as fast as possible, from your opponents. If you're in the middle of a negotiation, you must ask everything you want and respond to everything your opponent wishes to know so that everything's balanced.

You must make plans for the negotiation and know your opponents' plans. If yours are different to the counterpart's, you'll have to decide if you'll use them and also assess if this helps you or harms you. If the other party's plans inspire you trust, you can use them without any problems, but also making small changes as the negotiation moves forward.

If you deeply know your counterpart's plans, this is a point to your favor because then, you have more weapons to unbalance them in case that you feel like they're hiding information.

On the other hand, you can care for the information you supply and reveal it slowly. This is convenient in some cases.

The questions which manifest a tendency to a determined subject are seen as antagonistic and can cause a conflict.

Hypothetical questions are good to propose a solution which is beneficial for both parties. This is a quick way to negotiate.

Always try to start by the small business and move towards the big ones, or by the big ones and move towards the small ones, but you definitely must have an established pattern. The small businesses are quickly solved and the negotiation flows better. Something's that's also beneficial is solving the biggest business first, since this reduces the general anxiety and the rest of the negotiation moves with more ease.

Siempre trata de comenzar por los asuntos pequeños y avanzar hacia los grandes, o por los grandes e ir hacia los pequeños, pero en definitiva debe haber un patrón definido. Los asuntos pequeños se resuelven rápidamente y la negociación fluye más aprisa. Algo también beneficioso es resolver el asunto más grande primero, ya que esto reduce la ansiedad general y el resto de la negociación transcurre con más calma.

Intensification or exchange stage

In this moment it's when a point or business has increased, the parties are too involved and the offers are getting closer so that the objectives are fulfilled. You can use distraction, which is an attack to the weakest point of the opponent. What you must do is distract the attention from the strengths of the counterpart and attack their weaknesses. This tactic is a psychological game and is considered as fake and manipulative. If they try to use it against you, you must know how to identify it.

It's the most important thing in the whole negotiation, since in this stage is when the real exchange of concrete proposals happens. What is worth evaluating is what you're willing to exchange with the other party so that the agreement can happen. Sometimes you have to give something up to achieve greater benefits.

There are some tactics that you must apply during the negotiation process:

➢ **The non-negotiable and the bucket of cold water:** The tactic of the non-negotiable is used early on in the process. Its primary goal is to exclude from the negotiation any subject that has a great relevance to avoid future claims, so you don't think everything's lost in case you fail in it. If you get the counterpart to desist on these subjects, the negotiation would've been worth it and for moral matters within the agreement.

➢ **The paradise:** Just like the bucket of cold water the main objective of this point is bringing out transcendental subjects of the negotiation and adjusting to your favor the prevailing ones.

➢ **Divide and conquer:** Every member of the group must know in depth those subjects being treated on the table, but they're each granted with those which are more relevant to them and thus, the defense is much better against opponents.

➢ **Bad reputation:** Every conflict is unique; however, you can get quicker solutions if similar conflicts are studied. This way, the negotiation flows easily.

➢ **The Russian Front:** Everyone chooses what they will be fighting against, and this is a very good strategy because it allows them to defend themselves in what they like the most and what they know how to defend so they can achieve their goals.

> **The Brooklyn optic:** This tactic consists of setting a base sale price and then establishing a group of elements, as complements over the product, that are seen as profit by the buyer.

Closing or settlement stage

In this stage we have some tactics which are effective in the closure phase:

- **Create a time pressure:** You must find a way to not cause more meetings and ask yourself if you've already gotten what you wanted. If the answer is yes, you're on the right track of the negotiation.
- **Feint:** In negotiation, it is defined as arguing about another matter. After some negotiations about this new matter, the party which caused it must give in.
- **Revocation:** It's possible that a party revokes their previous approval about the first proposal as a response for not having gotten an agreement. This tactic can exert an effective pressure to achieve the closure.
- **Withdrawal:** In this tactic, the proposal being discussed is withdrawn. Sometimes it's done with the intention of making the other party want what it's being withdrawn. This sometimes work to close a negotiation.
- **Closing concessions:** You must consider doing them always trying to get something from your opponents.
- Silence: It's best to receive potential replies or questions than silence, since we don't know how to interpret it. If your counterpart says nothing, nor a yes or no, it's difficult to know what they're thinking.
- **Ultimatum:** When we say we don't see any viable alternative, is giving an ultimatum, but this is convenient to use only if you don't run the risk of breaking off the negotiations.
- **Retreat:** It's natural to not want to lose the nego-

tiation after having invested your time and energy in the process, but you must be prepared to retreat the moment you want to.

o **Creativity and patience:** You must know how to reply to questions in the best way, and know how to listen your opponent's answers, this will be helpful to move to the next stage in the most difficult part of the negotiation.

o **Small requests:** You can request some additional things that you believe can help you finish the negotiation. And save something to close the deal.

CHAPTER 12
MISTAKES IN NEGOTIATION

It's more convenient for the good to seem good than careful in their speeches.

(Aristotle, *Rhetoric*, 1418b, 1-2)

In a negotiation you mustn't act under any deceit or manipulation; you must study the pros and cons of the situations which affect the involved parties.

It's important that during the negotiation both parties are satisfied, even though, at times, the result isn't the expected. That's why, there's a series of mistakes that must be avoided so the communication is more pleasant, fluid and doesn't get worn out.

If you're not prepared, better not reply

Have you ever Heard the saying "it's best to be quiet and seem like a fool than speak and definitely clear up the doubts"? Well, it totally applies in this case. If it's necessary to postpone the dialogue to prepare a bit more, it's a more viable option than giving the other party the certainty that you're not ready to assume the negotiation and even facilitate tools they can use against you.

Don't try to reply just to get it over with, since you won't reach a good end and the negotiation would be pointless. Don't reply without being prepared about an important subject or matter simply because you hope that everything goes well, since you're not directing anything, simply reacting to a circumstance and you'll get worst settlements.

Don't gloat in your overconfidence

Oftentimes, it's thought that it's feasible, but it shows that there's a flaw in the logic or argument. Many people use more time trying to persuade the counterpart than creating a dialogue to know what the other person wants. We should not fail thinking that if an exposed argument doesn't convince us, it will convince the counterpart.

When we gloat in our overconfidence, more than intimidating the other person, what we do is making them defensive, irritate them, because they find it's a rather annoying attitude. Humility and empathy are the best weapons if you want to win enemy ground, don't play smart in front of the other party, this won't bring you anything positive.

Focus! Don't lose sight of your target

Don't focus on the profit or in what will the counterpart obtain. The primary thing is mutual benefit, without harming the other. What they will get is the counterpart of what you desire. The negotiator isn't born with talent, they prepare for it.

Having the discipline to be focused is one of the most difficult tasks to maintain, the primary thing is that the other attacks when they want to achieve their goals and unstable their strategies, bring you out of focus and put you at their will. You should be clear about what you want and don't lose sight of the preparation you've had to accomplish it, the satisfaction of getting your reward.

Don't assume that the goals aren't compatible

Both parties have different needs and values. You don't know what the counterpart wants. So, you might end up in a win-win situation when ending the dialogue. Paying attention to what the other person is expressing is important so you can know their arguments or their needs and try to reach an agreement that benefits both.

If you're going to negotiate with the predisposition that the things you both want are different, then you won't be able to focus on finding solutions which benefit you both equally. You must be a part of the solution, not the problem.

Don't pay too much mind to their weaknesses, focus on keeping a goal or a fixed plan of the main objective of the negotiation. Let's say that it's a low blow knowing the weak spots of the counterpart and try to have a benefit not by negotiating, but by blackmailing to get that information or leverage. It might not lead to anything in the future, since it wouldn't be beneficial for the other one. They would only accept by getting carried away by your arguments and you would be cutting a relationship with which you could've gotten better results further on.

Your arguments must be solid

Take a foundationless position or reasoning that doesn't contain a good backup and that it's not expressed in an assertive way to the other party is a common mistake, trying to defend or back-up a wrong position will make them reject it, discredit it and might even lead to conflict.

Keep in mind that if you can't back-up any point, it's because it isn't realistic or reasonable; don't waste time looking for arguments without a back-up, find a proposal that fits the goal of said negotiation.

If the other party presents you an irrational or non-assertive counteroffer, it's best to insist so that they back-up or correct said proposal or offer. You must keep in mind the personality of your counterpart, since it could be conceptualizing out loud the offer that isn't well defined yet. In this way, you could organize your ideas in the moment or realize what you're expressing or ask for a break to do so, and in the moment of the dialogue, define it correctly.

Establish the negotiation time

Make it clear from the beginning that you're pressured by a deadline that you must fulfill, there isn't something more exhausting than falling in the vicious circle of discussing the ideas without getting nowhere over and over.

Just like at times, it's recommended to be aware of the pressure that deadline imposes, it's also important to not feel forced so that everything flows naturally, but without losing sight of the established terms. There are alternatives, so you don't continue the negotiation if you feel under the pressure of a deadline. Avoid the characteristics of your personality to exert pressure on you.

The first offer can always be improved

Even if it might seem like a good one, it's really important to not jump right into the first offer they present to you. This doesn't mean you don't want to or don't want to accept the offer if it's appropriate, but, if you do it right away, you'd be taking importance or dignity away from the other person, and as a consequence they might recur to not fulfilling their end of the bargain in a future or feel unhappy.

The most recommended thing is to hide your enthusiasm, take the time to assess your proposal and correct lesser pending details. This attitude will grant you success for both parties and it will surely provide you with the opportunity to add points to the offer that weren't initially presented, being able to improve it considerably.

Don't give in too much, learn to say no!

You must learn to say no in an acceptable way, without criticizing, offending or blaming anyone. Having firmness is important, explain the reasons of your negative to any subject, using persuasion and assertiveness.

Don't give in too much, it might never be enough for the other party and they will ask for more and more thinking that they deserve it. Let's remember that good will causes greed instead of gratitude, this is a human reflection. So, if you're very generous, without getting nothing in return, you don't help the negotiation.

Avoid giving presents in this moment, since the other person is only thinking of themselves and your act will only be taken as weakness. Let's keep in mind that good will in a negotiation is born out of a good agreement and not from a gift.

If you need it, ask for a break

Knowing in what moment you can ask for a break is something you must learn to identify and request it without being ashamed of it. This is necessary, since you might check your information, think or consult something. In this way, you show the counterpart that you're tending to their points and thinking of their reasonings, you won't only be focusing in your own opinion, but you'll be taking into account what they've expressed and you'll assess it.

In the moment you feel blocked, and this happens frequently because in many negotiations they reach a point where they don't go anywhere, that's when a break is needed to calm the spirits and debate with less emotion. Just like when you need to consult with an expert about any aspect that comes up and which lacks information. But especially when you feel the strategy being used isn't the most appropriate it's necessary to ask for a break to review it.

Leave everything on record

When closing the negotiation, not making a summary

of the exposed objectives and not having the result of the agreement written down is a common mistake. It's not that you mistrust the other party's word, but there's nothing like the formality of the achieved to the care and benefit of both.

CONCLUSIONS

In conclusion, I can tell you that previous preparation to a negotiation is crucial to achieve success in it, not only for you but for the rest of the participants in the agreement.

Clear objectives and a good attitude are your best tools to start a dialogue. Also, it complements this with a detailed evaluation of the other party so you can recognize their interests and attitudes and be able to make assertive decisions about them. Don't let yourself be dominated by your ego, act humbly and with a great disposition to understand and be empathetic to the other person.

Negotiation is an art that is developed with a lot of study and discipline. All situations are different, so, more than learning everything like a recipe, what's best is opening your mind and develop abilities that will allow you to asses and respond in the best way of all parts involved.

Yes, there are people who have a certain ease at negotiation, but this doesn't mean that they're really effective when doing it.

We must always be preparing ourselves constantly, so that we achieve our goals and fulfill all the things that might make us happy and fill us with joy.

Negotiation goes beyond a merely professional term, we negotiate in everything and for everything, so why shouldn't we train this necessary skill. Yes, agreements don't always come out the way we want them to, in knowing these techniques there's the guarantee that we will be able to get the best agreement from the discussion and we'll promote relationships in the future with the other parties involved.

The best negotiator is that one who assesses the picture, has clear objectives, studies their opponent and puts into practice the strategies according to their goals with enough skill to convince the other one and without them feeling disrespected or impetuous during the process.

All negotiations require different strategies and attitudes. Being versatile and intelligent enough to achieve this is something that isn't simple, without a doubt, but it's not impossible.

It always comes from respect to others and starts by touching the simplest subjects and in which both have the same purposes, this is a good way of generating trust on the other party and soften the tone of the conversation.

According to the type and importance of the negotiation that you're planning, establish a deadline to achieve your goal. If you don't fulfill it, assess if it's worth it to insist in the process or simply retreat, with the conviction that this doesn't mean that you've lost; because in negotiations you don't go to win or lose, you go to reach settlements.

Negotiating is exchanging ideas to reach an agreement, always try that these agreements are properly documented and, if possible, with an endorsement which guarantees the satisfaction of both parties in the end, and that works as a signal that they both agree with what's been established. Remember that this, specially, applies to the professional area and to certain personal situations.

Effective communication must be the main pillar of strength when negotiating. How do you reach a settlement with someone without any communication? It's really impossible.

Another thing you must know how to handle is that not everything you set your mind to might be faithfully approved, so you must be willing to yield in some things. A negative, when it comes to this point, will turn everything more hostile and difficult when negotiating.

Understanding what the other party expects and how much you're willing to give in to please them and achieve your goals is fundamental to reach an agreement.

Qualities like flexibility, kindness, discipline, equality, respect and confidence are the main allies in the process of negotiation.

Define your target and study the other party, this will help you define the best strategies you can use to achieve your goals.

Remember each of the things you've read in this book and learn to put them into practice in a way that you become a skillful negotiator, without losing sight of the other party's interests.

I'd like to tell you how much Amazon ratings help me. Please rate this manual, and if it is possible, write your honest opinion about it. Comments help me improve and good reviews help increase the sales of this book, something that allows me to dedicate a little bit more time to writing. Thank you!

- Steven T. Walker

www.ingramcontent.com/pod-product-compliance
Lightning Source LLC
Chambersburg PA
CBHW070424220526
45466CB00004B/1527